Speak Destiny

A Powerful Path to Embrace Your True
Self, Overcome Negativity, and Find
Your Freedom

Brandi,

I am so excited to share my first book with you! Thank you for all you do to empower women. You are Black Girl Magic! I would love to hear your thoughts on my book and hope to one day connect! Continue being a light!

Speak. Believe. Do

Destiny Hilliard-Thomas

@iSpeakDestiny   SpeakDestiny.com

Destiny Hilliard-Thomas

Edited by Oyepeju Abioye and Tracy Avery
Book design by Iffy Creative
Cover photography by Atiba/5smphotos
Visual Styling by StylesbyLeek/5th Generation

Dedication

I dedicate this book to the amazing women in my life, specifically my tribe; my friends, sisters, and most importantly my mother-for it all, the grace the poise, and the humility. To my father for my firm foundation and tenacity. My husband for reminding me of my gifts and ensuring that I refrain from dimming my light. To my son for your patience and support as I continue walking in my purpose.

I also dedicate this book to women everywhere who are working hard to become the best versions of themselves; in spite of challenges stacked against them. We are our ancestors' wildest dreams!

Speak | Believe | Do

contents

Preface

Me and Acronyms

Mnemonics have always worked for me as a learner: they helped remind me of important facts. I can't remember a starting point, but in school, I learned *"Please Excuse My Dear Aunt Sally"* to remember the order of operations. It allowed me to latch on to the concept. In the order of operations, each mathematical symbol was represented by a letter, and when taking exams on such content, "PEMDAS" was an easy enough acronym to keep in mind and aid remembrance of the correct sequence of the steps.

As an adult, I have heard others use similar devices to present and retain information whether it be in the church, business, school or other environments. Having the acronyms in mind can spur your memory when you lose your train of thought.

Here's the exact point I'm trying to make: Most of us utilize mnemonics on a day-to-day basis without even considering what they are or realizing how dependent we are on them for effective functioning. We have become so used to them, that they are now enmeshed in our daily vocabulary and experiences. We have been taught things that become part of our toolkit even if we don't give credit to the source. I admit that

I do not always acknowledge sources prior to reeling out a fact such as stating that, "Like my grandmother always says," or "I recall my dad saying that..." While it is incredibly beautiful to reference the life lessons you have been provided, you might fall short sometimes- and that's okay too!

In this book, I will be presenting several examples and scenarios that I have been personally involved in, learned from, and grown from. From the situations I have been connected with or have helped others through, I create these scenarios that provide ultimate clarity and bring you to the point where you either make the choice of freedom or self-imprisonment. This book was written with ladies in mind: to invigorate, challenge and sharpen other women until they can look into the mirror and be exceptionally pleased with the woman, they see smiling back at them. Oftentimes, what keeps us from being the best version of ourselves is indeed, our very own selves. More times than not, we serve as double agents: sabotaging our own growth by being the barrier to our own prosperity, growth and ultimately, true freedom.

That sounds sad to hear, right? This is why I've written this book, so that the lion in you arises when you see how much of self-sabotage you've engaged in. If you are on board, I'd love for you to join me on this journey to freedom but be warned, some parts of this trip may be uncomfortable; some areas we go through may dredge up painful emotions and memories you'd rather keep buried, and remind us of hurt that we thought we were over (but really just bandaged), and highlight the aspects of our lives that can use some nurturing and attention. Keep this saying as a mantra: although the *process* may be very hurtful, it doesn't stop the *results* from being beautiful. My hope is that this process is transformational and that it does not end with you. I promise to be authentic and responsive throughout our journey while sharing some jewels that I have added to my crown along the way.

The purpose of this book is to be used as a tool to assist you on your road to self-discovery, identifying your purpose, and walking into the next amazing phase of your life. Each chapter details several strategies I've used successfully (after a fool-proof trial and error process). These strategies have also been used to help hundreds of others to reframe their thought process, dig deep within, and walk towards their calling. I hope that this becomes a guide for you and that you are prepared to put the work in. I can't do it for you, I can only provide you with the tools that I am confident will enhance your life and propel you into your next. Are you ready for the ride? Let's buckle up ladies! It is time to speak life, speak blessings, speak peace, speak change, speak healing, speak possibilities, speak growth, speak encouragement, and speak destiny.

My Creed

My work translates into a steadfast connection to an ideal. I believe in the people I work with. Your belief in self will take you as far or limit you as much as you allow it to. My belief in you as an individual and your impact—the vision and future I see— means nothing if you cannot see it for yourself. The seed may be planted by me, another, or yourself, but *you* make it grow. Once you grasp the belief that *you* have the power and the *freedom* to make it happen, the belief is manifested. Beliefs determine behaviors/actions and behaviors/actions are intended to meet a need. This means that all behaviors have meaning, purpose and intention behind it. What that meaning is the golden question and that is where much of the work takes place.

My impact is professional and personal. I have taught and counseled hundreds of youth and adults, who prior to our meeting, had shied away from education and due to self-doubt, were on the road to severe self-sabotage. From a point of perpetual worry about their futures, these amazing individuals became transformed positively, and now live awe-inspiring lives.   Of course, there was a process between those two realities: one where I consistently communicated to them the truth of my experiences; and how people just like them have succeeded- but it began with a mindset shift from the fixed "I can't" to the growth "I will...no matter what." With this kind of radical mindset shift, I have no inkling of doubt of their eventual success- regardless of which barriers are thrown their way to challenge their reality. You see, I have practical examples of students who have faced the judgement of having a criminal record or not completing school. Even after accomplishing what *others* said, they could not do, society attempted to derail them from living a life of self-satisfaction and belief in their accomplishment. Seeing such a picture challenges me to bring these students up to embrace their highest possible selves; so, I provide the outline while they paint the picture and together, we fill in the holes that life left them with. Quite heartbreakingly, these individuals have been so browbeaten by life into submission that at times, they feel that they are not worthy of living a life of peace and freedom, both physically and mentally; or they aren't the sort of people who should go to college or move beyond the station of their parents or toxic environments.

Many don't believe they are deserving or capable of simply thriving. The negativity causes holes, but belief and support create opportunities to become whole. The negative belief process that was previously ingrained in them begins to shift as the work begins. Understandably, it doesn't shift for all immediately. In fact, most people take quite some time before they are able to finally experience a radical shift in their way of thinking (mindset) because it is truly a *process*. Small successes create momentum.

Some of the most challenging students who resisted education and exhibited hostile and erratic behaviors would months later, end up as student leaders, high school graduates, college graduates, and even return after graduation to speak to students who are in the position, they once were. For me, this was extremely moving, and I would sometimes shed a tear or two, when I realized that again and again, people can be pushed into their destinies!

To give a background of the population I serve, many are living with mental illness, learning disabilities, addiction, homelessness, abandonment, abuse, and legal issues. This is both in my work as an educator as well as my work as a Mental Health Therapist. With all that had been set up to ensure their failure, and many negative seeds planted, the outcome had been mostly negative manifestations which then required countless hours of work, commitment and affirming the belief that better outcomes are possible; for there to be a reversal of those negative seeds. Subsequently, what each of them spoke and believed, good or bad, manifested.

As an educator, coach and therapist, I do not just pour into. I assess and also allow my students and clients to identify their intrinsic power to pull out and utilize the tools they already possess within, which have been lying dormant. I am not simply looking for them to make a change. I am assisting with their *transformation*. Yes, they are totally different terms: while change can be cold, rote, and stifling; transformation speaks to wholeness and growth—becoming the light you can be. Change will have someone doing what is required to receive a reward or the benefits of the right behavior. The transformation process, however, is so wholesome that it results in an individual speaking up when no reward is offered, partnering when no accolades are given, and responding to uncomfortable situations without conflict and outrage. Do you sense how fulfilling that is? The reward felt cannot be put into words that results from seeing a personal transformation and a torch being lit by a person who at one point, extinguished their own light Witnessing students support and inspire others after providing an intervention to empower and initiate their growth makes me speechless, at times bringing me to tears. This process leading to transformation isn't exclusive to the adults or adolescents that I work with on a day-to-day basis. True transformation is also available to you too sis! Let's get to it.

Speaking Destiny

For far too many of us, the reality of failure has been ingrained deeply; causing us to feel and believe it to be unescapable. It has been spoken, felt, and, observed in the lives of all who have experienced any form of trauma. As women, we carry this burden as a group - perpetuated by a pervasive societal expectation. Far too often, we feel that we must dim our light in order to not be the brightest person in the room due to the possible retaliation, in the form of subjection to harsh criticism, humiliation, comparison, judgement and discrimination.

As a black woman, this idea is further perpetuated as other stigmas come into play that many of our ancestors, for centuries, have felt forced to not only dim but mask their true selves in order to assimilate, accommodate, and avoid being identified as assertive, aggressive, loud, unprofessional, controlling and overall unqualified. Oh and of course the ever-present *"angry black woman"* trope. We are taught not to shine too brightly or bring too much attention to ourselves in order to be accepted while still being the best and working twice as hard, all with the mask of perfection.

The reality is that people are typically impressed and influenced by our grit, determination, resilience, power, fearlessness, and boldness. They just may not acknowledge it. They may respond with hateful retorts or vibe with us lovingly. Their response is not about *you* no matter what that response is. Walking in your truth and being free to be your authentic self is what matters. Your impact is what matters. That impact is about counteracting the reality of failure that is real in the lives of those who have experienced trauma. Let your tenacity, courage, strength and presence speak into existence a reality that allows people to see something in themselves that they did not see before. Let it allow you to awaken something within *yourself* that you weren't aware existed! (Trust me, it's in there).

In the same way that negativity is poured through multiple situations and dished out via unending channels, you must feed yourself positively. Just like when a body is full of infection, we work to introduce a cure. When there is poison in the body, we inject the antidote. Apply that same logic to your emotional, psychological, and spiritual health. For example, sign up for inspirational emails or texts. You must put in the actual work to reap the rewards of health. You cannot put in fast food and expect good health out. In the same way, you cannot ingest negative images, media, ideas and thoughts and expect perfect health as an outcome (Ever heard of "garbage in, garbage out?").

Change your playlist to speak to you with songs that repeatedly reinforce the notion that you are powerful and fearless. Granted, it will take some time for these messages to become beliefs but sis you have to trust the process and simply *begin*. Plant the seed and continually water it with positivity. You need to speak healing and wellbeing so that it grows. Speak consistently. A small match in a dark room will not lighten the whole room, but everyone in the room will know where the light extends from. This small light in darkness, although seemingly useless initially, has the power to light up every single match in that room without dimming or extinguishing its own light. We'll go deeper into this concept in a later chapter.

Generational curses and spiritual warfare, inherited depression, and generational grief are being passed down from generation to generation. Carrying this baggage, you become a "bag lady" due to no fault of your own. As women, many of us feel obligated to provide nurturing for others however we do not often direct that nurturing nature inwards. We neglect ourselves. Sadly, those of us that do get it right and practice self-care, implement boundaries, or simply put our wellness before the desires of others are questioned and called selfish, self-absorbed or "bougie."

The phrases I use were learned growing up in the church. I learned religion and routine and began a more spiritual journey as I became older. Yes, I am a Christian; I just put more of my focus on my relationship with God versus just the religious aspects of church. I believe that connection is what we all need. I am a spiritual person. For me, spirituality is not about religion as we know it today, but a true personal and intimate relationship with God, the Universe, ancestors or any connection one may have, that depicts spirituality. Spiritual warfare is not unique to people who count themselves as spiritual. You are not required to have a certain allegiance or background to feel the reality of the physical and spiritual world. Whether you call it God, the universe, or the atmosphere, you are responding to the reality of your experience, generational history, and perceived potential; and that's perfectly legitimate.

The shifts in the environment is not just physical. We now know, via years of research, that trauma becomes chemical and is transferred via gene expression on top of the traditional genetic expression. These are the phenotypes. They result from what we experience, generational history, and our perceived potential. This is called epigenetics. These create reality but also an opportunity. The spiritual weight you are carrying influences your response to and how you live in the world. Often, that spiritual weight becomes physical weight as we attempt to deal with trauma—abuse, rape, neglect, mental captivity, expectations, feeling that you have to be the savior or the peacemaker.

Women have been saddled with holding everything together, bottling up the anger, rage, and pain. We then reproduce children who have experienced these feelings in the womb. Do you see how this damaging cycle is perpetuated? It is therefore a matter of urgency for us to create enabling environments for ourselves to thrive, because if environmental changes do not occur, the cycle of negativity is reinforced and repeated. The solution is to gain freedom from the weight and transform the energy from oppressive to supportive.

The energy you put out is the energy you receive in response. It's really not complicated but it's also not immediate. You manifest the seeds that are planted from generation to generation. Generational blessings are possible. With this book, I am asking and providing the blueprint for you to shift the atmosphere—to transform your energy. You are who you are. You are also the person who may choose to break the generational curse. You can initiate the shift that trickles down and begins a *new* cycle. The generational blessings can and *will* be planted with you if you are intentional about repelling what has been. Not allowing history to repeat itself.

You have the power, the right, and the *freedom* to break the curse off your life, thus impacting the lives of your offspring and those connected to you. Now let me be clear, for those that are not familiar with terms such as generational curses. I'm not referring to a curse such as a magical spell but rather consequences or results of the sins/wrongdoings passed down through generations also known as generational trauma or generational cycles. Generational trauma can look like negative traits, behaviors, abuse or addictions that repeat generation after generation. It may in fact feel like you and your family are "cursed" or have "bad luck." I genuinely believe with everything in me that you and honestly everyone in your family, has the power to break free from history repeating itself. You can achieve beyond what the cycle suggested for you. The unsustainable patterns, learned behaviors, and reactions *can* stop with you. You begin to create new traditions, intentional choices, and responses that promote health and wellbeing.

We tend to either repeat or repel what we grew up seeing. We often don't choose to repeat the negatives, but where active choice comes in, is when we decide to *repel* the negative. When you look at the detrimental patterns, it is easy to do nothing and repeat. You must train your mind and make an *intentional* choice to repel the negative and turn the "curse" into generational blessings, health, healing, growth and freedom. I can't wait to show you how.

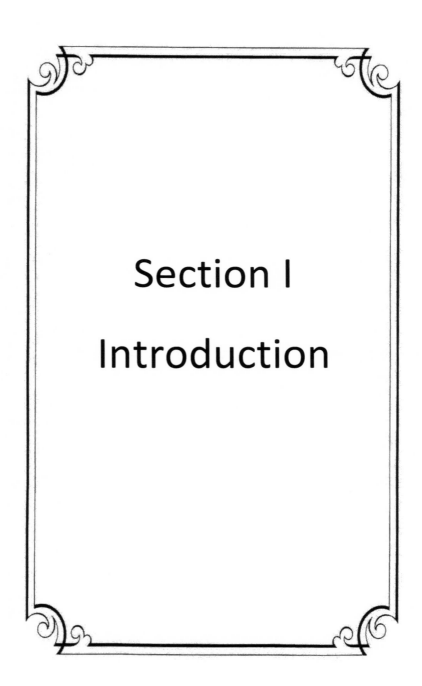

Section I

Introduction

Chapter 1
Societal Expectation

Perfection, Not Being

"She must be..." Society improperly applies unrealistic and unfair expectations and limitations on women's emotional, physical, and sexual freedoms. Music lyrics, videos, female body policing, politics, the entertainment industry (including casting) and media all show extreme judgement towards women.

This has caused many of us to feel as though we are on display, and that we *have to* fit in a certain checkbox of perfection, not only intellectually but also physically and emotionally. We must show up professional with every hair in place, but also balance that against not looking *too* sexy because that would warrant too much attention and possibly being blamed for the inappropriate comments, actions, or advances of our counterparts.

For years we have been given limited images of what the "ideal" woman is, what she looks like, her mannerisms, the number of children she has, her marital status and of course, how many sexual partners she has had. We have this deeply ingrained in our psyche, to the point where many of us have lost the core of our womanhood. Black women are specifically saddled with these challenges, alongside having to worry about the negative stereotypes attached to our naturally bestowed features (nose, lips, hips, hair texture) and skin color. If that isn't enough, black women have to deal with not only these racially charged judgements and expectations but also the issue of colorism within our own community from both men and women.

Too often, black women are at the forefront of activism for several marginalized groups, however we have become accustomed to not having support when we fight for our own emancipation. We have been expected to show up, rally and support many groups, but how many of the aforementioned groups consistently show up when black women chant a battle cry to specifically emancipate black women? Sadly, not so many show up for black women, even within movements that are designed for women.

I personally identify as a feminist however, historically, the separation of the plights of black and white women in the movement and the suffering of black women has neither been uniquely highlighted, nor deeply supported. We see this continue to play out even in society's response to victims of abuse. There is a separation of who is believed by society (not only the justice system) and who is lying for "clout" or should have known to leave to prevent sad realities from occurring. The sympathy and outrage received simply do not align. This is not to say that women as a whole are not dismissed or taken seriously.

We cannot discuss the challenges of all that women go through as a collective without identifying the specific challenges that women of color experience in this country as being that of both women and women of color. The intersectionality of black and female is exponential. This goes even deeper with being an LGBTQIA+ woman of color. It seems as though the more minority checkboxes you check off, the experiences and masking are magnified due to society's vision and identification of a "true woman." Classy, beautiful, natural, sexy but also wholesome, moral and virtuous, a present mother, a doting and faithful wife, submissive but still smart and opinionated, and educated. These are just a portion of the conflicting identities that many women have felt or still feel they have to adhere to, so as to not only feel accepted but to also feel worthy. Ladies, this should not be so; none of these variables define you as a woman! Take the mask off and reintroduce the unmasked you to YOU. Then introduce yourself to those around you, taking immense pride in the woman that you are and are working on becoming.

While wearing the mask to oblige to society's standards of being a woman (which has forced many of us to believe that there is a specific image of beauty, actions, and beliefs), millions of women have been willing to risk their lives and natural selves to adhere to an at best, opaque standard of beauty. Whether that includes deadly butt injections done by non-professionals, skin lightening creams/treatments to be a lighter tone (as society shows/tells us the lighter the better), perms, weaves, makeup, any other extreme enhancements to simply connect with what we are shown, told and sadly believe about the definition of true beauty. Now, before this is taken out of context, let me make a disclaimer. I am by no means saying there is an issue with anyone straightening their hair, wearing makeup, weaves or even enhancing your physique through plastic surgery. What I want you to explore is the background reason behind any changes you make. Is it for YOU or to make the mask permanent? I encourage women to make enhancements that suit their own preferences and the freedom of being, not to assimilate, accommodate, or adjust to the expectations of what others have said you should look like, wear, and behave as.

There is a major difference between freely doing and freely following. Take some time to sit with that if you will. What does that mean for you? Being a woman is a beautiful thing and I wouldn't trade my experiences as a woman for anything. Okay maybe a cramp here or there but you get it. What we as women should identify as #goals are being our true selves, ridding ourselves of the idea of what we are told we as women are and just being. Whatever that is for you. Learn yourself enough to know what and who you are and be free and confident in that. THAT my dear are true #goals. When you can truly free yourself from the expectation of others and just do you boo! This is something I am truly passionate about.

Many of us are masking until we can't anymore. Women are not monolithic. Yet certain norms are central to the culture and certain experiences are integral to being identified as a true woman of worth. As a matter of fact, queen status is too easy to lose for women, an idea that we need to separate from. We adopted the belief that a woman must respect her body and herself in order to deserve respect, receive love, be deemed as worthy, the list goes on. Society, men, even other women have told us what respecting one's body looks like and how it should be done in order to be worthy enough for a true love, marriage, respect and semi equality. For example, a woman of worth isn't expected to engage in certain acts, even when she wants to. As such, many women have rejected self-truth to be considered worthy- a status that is snatched away once she shows any sense of deviation from the perceived standard.

The challenge is that this has resulted in a refusal to talk about certain aspects of our lives. Women clutch their pearls and say that they are not involved in sexual exploration. Women often feel the need to reduce numbers while men are free and encouraged to inflate their numbers. Ladies, true self love comes from having freedom within to simply be. If that looks like sweats and sneakers on the outside, great! If that looks like getting dolled up just because and wearing 6-inch heels with a see-through crop top, amazing! If that looks like a turtleneck with a belted skirt, awesome. If that looks like using profanity when you speak and listening to ratchet music, I'm here for it. Do you sis! But whatever you do and exhibit on the outside, do so because your inside is free to express, eliminating any of the expectations and limiting beliefs that your worthiness can be purchased at a department store. Don't do any of it based on external pressure or a craving for acceptance.

One major problem with putting a mask on is that you forget that you have the mask on. You can lie for so long that the lie meshes into your identity. It becomes challenging to know who you authentically are. We become what others need us to be. By adopting this faux reality, we inflict harm on ourselves.

As women we are judged by a mindset that says that we must pour out for everyone else and leave nothing for ourselves. But what can you honestly pour out from an empty glass? "As long as your kids and husband are set, you are a real woman." We have adopted a stance that suffering and sacrifice are the standard of greatness. And don't get me started on "struggle love"; women sacrificing themselves, goals included, to help build up, repair and care for an emotionally bruised significant other while drowning and neglecting themselves. Sis, that's not love, that's toxic attachment! Many of us attach to someone based on "trauma bonding"; attaching to the broken, unhealed and toxic areas in others that we identify with and somehow feel as though we can "cure" the toxicity while in fact, it generally exposes and magnifies our own unhealed areas and drowns us in their brokenness-continuously making effort to "fix" the other while neglecting ourselves. Keep in mind, a Queen is still a Queen, with or without a King. The lack of a man or woman in your life doesn't take away one bit of your royalty. Our greatest goals and accomplishments in life shouldn't be tied to another adult; but rather something that we created, birthed (spiritually or physically). We view singleness as a curse and marriage (happy or unhappy) as the ultimate goal and true definition of being and feeling complete. Imagine being and feeling complete with YOU before AND after getting joined in marriage, a committed relationship or friendship? How awesome would that be; to align with someone that adds to you but doesn't complete you because the only way to complete something is if it is unfinished, not whole. You are not just enough; you are more than enough!! I dare you to believe it sis- with the whole of your being.

Too often we ensure we are the last to get cared for and have done our duty as women to properly care for everyone *but* ourselves. We neglect our health to put others first, and then have the nerve to brag about it. That's not healthy or boast worthy. You must understand that you cannot provide the best care for anyone if you are not healthy and whole yourself. You cannot be the best wife, girlfriend, friend, employer/employee, mother, or leader if you are not healthy yourself. When I speak of health, it is inclusive of mental, physical, spiritual and emotional health. Struggle mentality tends to get praised while the inalienable truth of our queenship is denied in our everyday action and understanding. If this is you, you deserve more! You are worth more. You should expect and demand more and if not received, move on to where you are celebrated and not tolerated. Search the areas within where you haven't healed, where you've been exposed unwillingly, where you have experienced trauma, where you are masking pain with the façade of "strength". You deserve wholeness, healing, freedom. Begin the process.

I want you, Queen, to exhibit an illuminous glow causing others to inquire about what's taking place in your life. Women often comment about the glow they see when they look at a woman who is pregnant or has a special life event, but I challenge you Queen to begin working on your glow. Your natural glow. One that exudes just because you are confident in your wholeness and walking in your freedom, not solely because of an extension of you such as a baby, a relationship or a promotion. Don't wait for a momentous occasion or life altering event to occur to show your glow. Work on it daily. Be so focused on your glow up people ask, "girl you must be in a new relationship or pregnant because you are glowing!!!" Respond with "nope, not at all. That's just wholeness. I'm walking in my freedom!" The glow will come from the heart work and soul work. Not only do we provide a false or improper example of adulting, but we also validate a lack of self-love. When you do not make yourself and your health a priority and give from that position, you set up your children and those you influence to put themselves in a secondary position in favor of some other person thus making room for a cycle to begin (or continue).

Last summer, I came across an article by a former bail bondsman that revealed that in all his years working as a bondsman, most of the people addressing bail bonds were women. No matter their financial situation, they put themselves and their finances on the line to bail out their loved ones. He said it was basically encouraged by attorneys to contact the women versus the men connected to the inmate. They stated women, especially mothers and girlfriends, were more likely and willing to give up what they had, for someone else's freedom whether it was a home, cash, or loans. He included one scenario where a woman bailed out a man who was accused of assaulting minors with the reasoning that, "My children need a father." We must discontinue these damaging and toxic cycles, ladies. No, not all women fit these specific examples I have provided but far too often, women, seem to be willing to sacrifice our own for the betterment or even freedom of someone else in the name of love, friendship, Godliness, whatever. Be free queen, be free.

Gender Roles

Being 10 times as good for half the acknowledgment is often the sad reality for women especially within the workforce, including entertainers. Generally, the expectations are not the same for women and men. We know that, but the responses to women that have any perceived difficulty are troubling. I remember attempting to hide my pregnancy during a job interview. I got the job and revealed my pregnancy when it was no longer possible to conceal my baby bump.

It was Summer by that time and the expectation on the job was to work an additional 10 hours per week. My supervisor at the time was really kind. She stated, "If you need to stop at 40, that is acceptable due to your pregnancy."

I insisted on "going hard" and meeting the expectation just like everyone else. I worked up until my last week before the birth. The thought process for me was that I must prove that a woman can do the job as assigned, without limits, without excuses. I did not make the connection that this choice of mine was a trauma response. On introspection, we'd discover that many decisions that we make solely based on the view, opinion or acceptance of someone else, is often a trauma response and we rarely identify it. It was only recently that I was able to process the difference between perfection and excellence. My pregnancy became painful during my last two weeks (my son shifted to my sciatic nerve). The pain was real sis! My husband encouraged me to decline the increase in work hours, and to begin my leave so that I would be comfortable and not push myself too hard. My supervisor was also supportive. However, I could not see that I had that freedom to decline and also step down. I was always so used to taking on more in every aspect of my life to help others, especially professionally. I could not see that hard, grueling work was not the only way to approach my career. Thankfully, I took that last week off and my child was delivered...and then hours after he was born, I was in labor and delivery with my laptop completing postgraduate assignments for the 12 additional credits I took that summer in order to become eligible for the National Counseling Exam to become a Mental Health Therapist. I was really doing the most and of course my husband was trying to get me to relax, telling me the professors know I just had a baby and that I deserved and needed to rest and relax. I couldn't see it that way. I didn't want a "pass" due to having a baby. Again, trauma response. You might have recognized any of these responses in your own life.

There is an episode of *Girlfriends* (season 1 episode 16) where Tracie Ellis Ross' character Joan Clayton was being dismissed when she provided ideas to her firm. In one episode, she lost her cool and stormed out. Someone commented that it must be that time of the month rather than identifying the blatant disregard and disrespect that had consistently been meted out to her. She came back to another meeting and attempted to speak in a male voice to demand the respect and attention she deserved. She continued experiencing these challenges throughout her tenure there as the only black woman (until several seasons letter when another black woman joins the firm as Senior Partner). Later on in this episode, Mr. Swedelson introduces a client (Mr. Darden) and refers to Joan as a young associate. Here's how it plays out:

Mr. Swedelson: "This is Joan Clayton, one of our bright, young associates."

Joan: "Nice to meet you. I'm actually a junior partner now."

Mr. Swedelson responds, "Oh really, when did that happen?"

Joan: "About six months ago. You gave me the promotion..."

The episode highlighted the reality that many of us feel and have experienced within the corporate world as either women or women of color. Have you ever had moments (or witnessed) where you were overlooked while someone who re-suggested your ideas was acknowledged? Have you been the only woman in the room and thought to be "granted" your position to "diversify" the environment rather than earning your position there? I hope you haven't but the reality is that it is far too common an experience- so much that it has become a shared trauma for women to bond over, leaving us emotionally overwrought. It is as if we must embody perfection which creates the profile of the mask. It appears that boys are nurtured and loved while girls are raised and prepared.

In the workplace, for the holidays, women are asked what they are cooking while men are asked about what their wives are cooking. Men decline invitations for after-work stating that they must babysit, while women are not invited due to the expectation that they must parent. And we unwittingly, subconsciously often wear this reality as a badge of honor and confirmation of our worth in society. The weight of this is heavy and heavier as the years progress and the differentiation between men and women in the workplace becomes more obvious.

The Standard of Freedom

The quote states, "...I could have freed a thousand more if only they knew they were slaves." Harriet Tubman did not say it, but the point made by a popular quote erroneously attributed to her is clear and valuable. You must find the awareness and courage to realize your oppression and act to overcome it. The comfortable space for women is ever-changing and always oppressive in that the target is always identified by others. You know that you are not free when you are operating outside of your comfort zone. In my example, I was pregnant and asked to work another 10 hours above the normal expectation. This loudly screamed against my comfort, but my internal discussion with myself was that I didn't want to appear incapable or to be challenged by others who would compare their ailment to mine. When you are provided with options and decline those options solely because of the judgments of others (often, these are perceived judgments), then you are not operating from a position of comfort and instead, you are acting from a position of perceived judgement. We think of ourselves as selfish, but we must provide the same selflessness to ourselves that we apply to others.

Selflessness is praised in our society. We give awards to humanitarian individuals and organizations who give of themselves. You must differentiate selfishness from being stingy. The selfishness that is characterized by self-care, health, peace of mind, putting yourself first and a true glow is acceptable. Greedy selfishness, self-protection, and disregard for others is not what we should aspire toward. The temporary glow of life events must give way to an experience of positivity that is consistent, long-lasting, and renewable.

Freedom is freedom from the judgments and expectations of others. When you feel inhibited or stifled by the thoughts and feelings of others, how can you call that freedom? As a matter of fact, you are far from being free. The limitations that others put on you, the comparisons, the what-ifs, and the criticisms must be laid aside for freedom to truly take hold. It is not just positivity that we are concerned with. It is not just an elevation of mood. I want an awareness of wholeness. In this, you are operating regardless of the external factors. In spite of any external conditions, you are operating with all pieces intact. This is the soul work.

I remember the story of a mother who lost her son. He was her all. He had just completed kindergarten and was preparing for first grade. That piece of her heart is still missing, but she recovered and identified her light even though that amazing extension of herself is gone. She discovered a way to move forward into a new normal. She freed herself from the identity that was tied completely to motherhood. She developed an identity within herself. She had to not only to survive but to thrive. She didn't get over it, she got through it.

If you are free to be - rather than struggle to be perfect, you must understand what it means to hold an identity outside of your relationships with others. The titles that you hold are an identity that is tied to others. Mother, Student, Employee, Sister, Wife...these are tied to what you do or your relationship to others. If these titles are the culmination of all of whom you are, if that represents your sole being, then you do not have anything worthwhile to contribute to those roles. Without the externals, what would be your definition of self? You need to exhibit intrinsic qualities such as: Sensitive, Intuitive, Creative, Spontaneous, Charismatic, Attentive...the list is vast and variable. These represent wholeness. Your experience of these is self-awareness and a foundation for self-expression. Your application of these is freedom.

Reflection Questions
1. What masks are you wearing?
2. Think about times you felt that you had to shrink yourself in order to be accepted or heard.
3. How often have you limited your desires in order to meet the limitations presented by society?

Chapter 2
Damaged
Relationships

Our last chapter discussed your identity and the social pressure to conform to extrinsic standards that don't necessarily encompass whom you are on the inside. Your identity outside your relationship with others (i.e. your own definition of whom you are) is a critical first revelation in your quest to Speak Destiny. The second revelation concerns your relationships with others and the meaning, influence, and resilience you gain or lose in interaction with your social influences.

Iyanla Vanzant's show, *"Fix My Life"* is one that readily comes to mind as I look for a good enough description of what I'd like to express. I remember one episode with the family of LisaRaye. There were 3 generations on the show. They could see the dysfunction, but they were unable to identify how to fix it or to even take the first step- which was to discuss the dysfunction perpetrated over the years, while taking accountability. Iyanla pointed out that neither generation of women would take responsibility for what they continued to display within the family interaction.

"I wish it were you." The fact of hearing things put on the table as real and being forced to deal with it was incredibly painful. Viewers didn't get a happy ending, as the sheer toxicity and damage on display were not repaired at the time of the show taping. Neither of them had considered that the mother was fighting for the motherly role with her daughter and the respected wife role with her late husband. Iyanla offered that the husband played both the mom and the daughter, by placing the daughter in the role of a "side chick" in the eyes of the mother. The mother and daughter passed this dysfunction down to their adult granddaughter who didn't even know the origin of the "mess" but was very much a participant in the dysfunction at play. Another issue that the mother had was that the daughter, LisaRaye, was not appreciative. She complained that LisaRaye should be indebted or at least appreciative. That burden, Iyanla points out, is not appropriate for a daughter mourning her father.

The challenge of healing is difficult anyway, because even the toxic becomes comfortable. Again, because we sometimes are unable to separate the roles or titles a person holds, we cannot determine how others should feel in an interaction. We sometimes cannot recognize the brokenness or need of others. We instead seek our comfort and safety. Too often, we expect and become too accustomed to trauma being a part of the experience. It becomes normalized. Those experiencing the trauma don't seek help to process and overcome. How can you seek help for what you don't assess or view as a problem? It's quite damning. Most people expect people to be a title (mother, father, grandmother, grandfather, aunt, uncle, cousin, supervisor, Principal, teacher, etc.) with a set of responsibilities regardless of their hurt, damage, and trigger. Children with unresolved and unaddressed trauma grow up and become adults, at least physically. Emotional growth doesn't simply manifest due to turning eighteen. Many of us have experienced the trauma of being raised by adults who were emotionally still in adolescence or even childhood. The Psychiatry Department at Harvard University conducted a research study and concluded that childhood trauma can stunt growth in parts of the brain preventing emotional and mental growth and maturity. Understanding this can help us understand some more of why we experienced certain responses, behaviors and abuse from those who actions didn't align with the set of responsibilities associated with that title. Does knowing any of this reduce the pain, make it fair and justified? No sis. However, what it does is it allows us to view those who have recycled their own trauma with a level of compassion. We can truly see them for whom they are: flawed people who needed to be protected, secure, safe, and loved, just like you needed to be. With this level of compassion and awareness, you are better prepared to be the vessel that would put an end to the negative generational cycle in your family. Yes, this cycle can end with you and generational healing can begin through you.

Triggers

My grandmother was not the typically affectionate grandmother. She was old school for real. You could get in trouble for getting a drink of water or juice during dinner and her words at times could pierce your soul. Her story is one that would not suggest her as a vulnerable and emotional person. It took me a while to understand what my grandmother went through and how pain and trauma changes a person. It is difficult for a child to understand, that a parent or grandparent would not be loving and nurturing. The challenge I had when recalling unpleasant memories with her was to transition from thinking "What is wrong with her?" to "What happened to her? Why does it seem as though pain is all she knows and shows at times?" Interestingly, no matter how much unhappiness she showed to people, she showed the opposite towards her plants. She had several plants throughout her house, especially in the living room by a large window. I can't recall any specific names for them, but I do remember that she was consistent with tending to them, providing the necessary nutrients so they would flourish. It was something she enjoyed, something she controlled, something that brought her peace, and ultimately, something that couldn't harm her or cause her pain or disappointment. As an adult reflecting back on those moments that I didn't understand as a child, I get it. I have a better glimpse into all the internal battles she was fighting that she masked with a tough exterior. I was always so curious as to how it seemed like she could transition to such a calm, affectionate, and patient woman with her plants but become extremely impatient, frustrated and angry at people, even children without any reason, at least from my point of view as a child.

Learning so much more about my grandmother as an adult provided me with a different lens. I went from being upset and disappointed for so long at some of what she had done and those that I love that she hurt, to feeling deep compassion for her. I was able to see the unprotected and abused woman that created a mask which included a tough exterior, protecting her from any further hurt and pain. I was able to see past her title of grandmother and see a woman; a broken, bruised and battered woman who did her best to move on with the pieces she was able to recover. When she passed away, I was not in a good space with her due to some inaccurate information she shared which was painful to not only me but other close family members. Years later I grew in certain areas and forgave her and even became apologetic for not understanding her pain, her triggers, and her trauma responses. Although she was deceased by the time I came into this space, I was able to release and free myself of the resentment and pain I had bottled up and allow for healing and forgiveness to take place in my heart. This only happened when I viewed her life through a compassionate prism. I was only a teenager when she left this earth, but it was years later as an adult that I was truly able to *see* her...beneath her mask, beneath her yelling and tough exterior. I saw the unprotected, damaged and hurting girl within her presented as a strong woman. I've worked with several clients who share similar backgrounds as my grandmother, who reveal their most intimate parts of themselves to me and share the areas they wish to improve upon or discover areas they didn't realize had caused great impact. Many times, my mind goes back to my grandmother; how I wished that she had the opportunity to reach out and seek therapy or even openly talk to loved ones and close friends about her deep-rooted pain and trauma. I wish we also had the opportunity to address the pain she inflicted onto others due to her own pain and trauma and any pain she felt she received from any of us. Unfortunately, these opportunities cannot become reality however, the healing, processing, forgiveness and growth can and did, for me. I was intentional. It was holding too much weight, emotional weight that I was no longer willing to carry forward, and so I dropped the baggage. When we are able to see past our loved ones' titles and expectations, we can begin to learn more about their make-up, and this ultimately provides   more clarity about certain behaviors and responses to their own trauma. It helps us with the *why* but doesn't necessarily correct the pain we experienced as a result of their actions or inactions. Often times, our caregivers/parents/elders are growing, learning and coping at the same time we are. Many are trying to heal the traumatized and wounded child within, while presenting themselves as adults who have it all together. This is a mask which we are all too familiar with, a dichotomy of sorts. We don't and shouldn't have to understand and process these dynamics as children, however, in order to process our own trauma as adults, often times suppressed, and move towards healing, it is important to look beyond the title of those we have damaged relationships with whether it be with a parent, grandparent, sibling, cousin, or aunt/uncle and see the individual. The flawed, damaged, broken, abused individual who transferred their pain undeservingly to you. Refuse to take responsibility for the undeserving treatment you experienced; it wasn't your fault. You are however responsible for getting through it, your healing, growth and becoming free from the bondage from these experiences. Your freedom is your responsibility. To become free, you need to identify what has held you in captivity. Be specific and be honest with yourself. It will hurt, it will be uncomfortable, but it is necessary in the journey to releasing past pain, hurt and becoming free.

There is no one-size-fits-all approach to working with someone who has not addressed nor identified their trauma or sorted through their "baggage." Sometimes, people are not open to hearing or addressing the trauma that they have experienced. Children who grow up into adults don't naturally recognize how trauma informs and even structures their choice of behavior. They adapt. They survive. Yet, you can set a tone and create a healthy environment. Rather than bringing something in confrontation, another approach may be to allow conversation in the context of a safe environment. Don't engage to "win", engage to understand with compassion. Engage to heal. Engage to forgive. Engage to become free.

Often, the brunt of a parent or caregiver's anger and frustration is displayed towards their children simply because they are easier targets. They are present, innocent and have unconditional love for their parents, regardless of whether they feel it in return. Sometimes, it is because children are the ever-present reminders of the challenges that parents face. "If it wasn't for you..." is the statement attached to a sense of regret or felt resentment. When addressing these triggers of others, ensure that you check if you are the recipient of a trigger reaction, make sure that you are not perpetuating a trigger reaction yourself. Ensure that you are not hurting others out of a need to address your own hurt. You know the saying, "hurt people hurt people." Identify what, if any, unintentional (or even intentional) trigger reactions you may be displaying towards those you love. Take a stance of complete honesty with yourself. This is not easy. Lord knows it isn't. But being honest with yourself is a part of the process to setting yourself free from emotional, spiritual and mental bondage.

One interesting intervention could be the usage of flashcards with attention placed on positive interactions and an adequate healing language. This method allows each individual to write down and share their love as well as the areas of pain they have experienced. There should be a card for each person included in the intervention, not a solo intervention as that can feel like an ambush, therefore, limiting progress. It is important to set ground rules when beginning this activity: no walking off, no yelling, everyone should be open to hear truths from their loved ones, no belittling or condescending due to disagreeing with what another member is saying. In these moments, it's important to allow each person to share their truth, their perspective, their reality. Our feelings are ours and our experiences shape our story. Invalidating each other's feelings or experiences will inhibit the healing process and limit growth. These rules need to be implemented at the beginning of the activity. State the intentions of the activity, being clear that the major objective is to gain understanding, gain perspective, ask or offer forgiveness, and become free from generational cycles and trauma. Often, this type of intervention requires a professional so that they do not devolve. Each one of us (including you sis) can begin to process healing one sit-down, one conversation at a time. Again, it will be uncomfortable but so healing, freeing and necessary.

Remember that the process of self-reflection is a critical one. Some people say the phrase, "Date yourself." Pay attention to what you do, how you react, situations that shift your mood, triggers that make you go off. Did you feel small, embarrassed, less than, or threatened? If you feel belittled or called out, it may connect you to and remind you of a previously buried memory from childhood that made you feel the same way. This is called a trigger because the memory is always there, even if suppressed, a present occurrence can cause a certain emotion. That emotion connects to a past experience where we felt that emotion and *triggers* an emotional response, an unhealthy response. This is also referred to as a trauma response. You may not have responded with anger or acting out in the original memory, but in this trigger moment, you may respond in the way that you desired to respond in that prior experience but felt powerless or felt numb at that moment. Present reactions due to triggers tend to be magnified, more intense than the situation suggests appropriate. When triggered, we are not responding to the present situation, but the memory connected to that emotion which generally has nothing to do with the person who is receiving our emotional response.

I suggest that you keep a journal of the times when you are triggered. Identify the memory that feeling connects with. Often, it is a feeling of inadequacy or a lack of control. Walkthrough the process of recognizing your choice opportunity and the control that you possess. You can respond rather than react. You can respond with intentional action rather than the emotion-laden reaction of the prior experience. This is a process that requires intention and mindfulness. If you are unaware of your triggers and unable to identify triggers and unhealthy responses, you are blocking yourself from addressing the root of the trigger. The past trauma, pain, hurt. You deserve healing. You deserve freedom. You deserve to respond to any situation in a healthy way that benefits you long term rather than reacting in a manner than can be detrimental to your job, career, education, future, or even your happiness.

Your Own: Repeat or Repel

Repeating and repelling are the options. Repelling is often a choice made by an intentional person recognizing that something was presented or patterned that was unsustainable. They decide to make a change toward greater sustainability. Repeating is often not a choice. When you do not know any better, when you don't have a more sustainable example for comparison, you repeat the experience.

I have witnessed people in abusive relationships that celebrate the experiences that they have in the experience of abuse; talking about the joy felt in reuniting with the abuser and feeling that the past experiences were necessary to get to where they are now. Sis, if this is you, know that you deserve better. You must come to the realization that trauma isn't a prerequisite for love. Struggle love needs to be outlawed. The ride or die mentality must die when it involves normalizing hurt, pain and struggle in a relationship to prove your love and "loyalty." When kids are present, they observe the "horseplay," the "tough love," and the "accidental bruising." The children learn that this is the way relationships work. They then grow to accept relationships (or even expect relationships) to have an abusive component as well as unlimited forgiveness. They can adopt the believe that "pain is love." Would you really want that for your kids? I wouldn't think so.

The first thing people ask when a child or young adults acts out is, "What was going on in their home?" We ask that because our minds are a canvas when we are young. Whatever is painted on that canvas is the truth and reality. Without an opportunity to be informed, they may continue to believe, react, and live within what could be a complete fabrication.

The "Repeat and Repel" processes are critical because your ability to reframe and attain higher heights in self-awareness hinges upon the opportunity to look backward, comprehend the reality and process, and make new choices. If you do not process through the pain and compare it to more sustainable realities, you will repeat those patterns. I am not a fan of "once an addict always an addict" because I do believe that people can transform and a past addiction should not be a lifelong identity once clean. I do however realize the application of this phrase in the context of triggers. You have a propensity to return to those things that you experienced in the past. Understand the situation and the context that led up to it. Awareness is an asset in itself. You can't fix anything unless you are aware. Creating this opportunity for intentionality is how you repel and move forward on your journey to becoming a newer, more improved version of yourself. An example of repel or repeat are two siblings who grew up with an abusive father who was also an alcoholic. One sibling marries the love of his life, intentionally does not drink and treats his wife like the queen she is, showering her with unconditional love and affection. He became this type of husband because of his experience having an alcoholic, abusive father. His brother however has been in and out of work due to his drinking, frequently taking out his anger from life's issues out on his girlfriend both emotionally, mentally and physically. He became what he saw, what he learned. He repeated the cycle, even though he despised what he witnessed! Think about the key areas in your life. Are you repeating or repelling certain patterns you have experienced?

Reintroductions

Here's a salient question: "How do we reintroduce ourselves once we are on the path to becoming?" When others attack you for the old you, that is not your issue. What is at stake here, is the reality of your relationships. You will find that your circle will change when you begin to grow. How often have you seen butterflies walking on the ground with caterpillars? Tyler Perry promoted the analogy in his book of the types of people who come into your life. Some people are leaves, some are branches, while others are roots. You will lose leaves as seasons change. Branches will connect you to other opportunities. Your core are those relationships that are rooted- who completely refuse to be swayed by the wind or even trauma. Root friendships are solid, throughout any season, storm, or sunshine, the roots are consistent and present. Leaves are supposed to fall off dependent upon the season and environmental changes.

Understand that a critical experience of healing is to comprehend that letting the leaves go does not have to result in a dramatic exit. Losing contact, reducing the frequency of contact, and finding new interactions will occur naturally. Sometimes, the losses are not losses at all. Sometimes, they are the challenges and trauma that held you back and kept you sick. Sometimes, those that fall away are great and excellent in their own unique ways, they were just not compatible with your direction and success. Be okay with the seasons' changing, even if you didn't see the prediction. Many of us are unable to get well because we are still connected to what got us "sick" in the first place. We are unhappy, yet comfortable in our sadness. Allow the leaves to fall! Allow the branches to connect you to where you need to be. Be grateful for the roots that remain, weathering all storms, never uprooting.

The famous month-long study by the Royal Horticulture Society demonstrated that talking to plants positively helps them grow. It is something that I promote in my own life. I never want to be a person that enters a room and sucks the energy from it. I want to improve the lives of others when I enter a room or an interaction. I also want to frequent environments where I am fed by others rather than drained by their interactions.

Two things come to mind. The first is the challenge of leaving people behind—the fear of letting go. This is the same as the fear of failure. It is the challenge of accepting that some people will say that you think you are too good, or you think you are better than them.

"There is freedom waiting for you in the breezes of the sky. And you ask "What if I fall?" Oh, but my darling, what if you fly?"

-Erin Hanson. You can always say what if the worst happens? Instead, you can re-channel that energy to also ask: "what if I fly?" I challenge you to the what-if. If they leave you, consider that you were better off without them.

The second is the fear of maintaining this new person you are. I want to remind you that this change is not about looking good to other people. It is about becoming the best you. If you fear embarrassment or judgement, you can switch that to ask, "How can I continue to improve along this journey?" You know that you need to become whole. The validation of others isn't your primary concern. You disconnected from that need when you reintroduce yourself. Keep making progress!

Reflection Questions
1. What relationships are feeding my joy and progress?
2. What relationships are draining my joy and progress?
3. If I overcome fear and celebrate my daily progress, what could I achieve?

Chapter 3
The Art of Failing

The path to your greatness may look hideous. If you think you are going to be successful the first time around, you are in for an awakening. This awakening can either be rude or expected. Anyone who has succeeded will tell you that they had to fail to understand how high they could go. If you win the first time, your success peaks. You know one who climbs, not by the heights attained, but through what they have overcome. Failures are opportunities for intense self-reflection and observation. These actions are again, an emphasis on individual identity and interaction with others. Take the time to evaluate yourself and your trajectory. Next, review your influences, past and present, and feed your growth, potential, and momentum.

The Last Dance highlighted how Michael Jordan created relationship challenges to get himself riled up for games. The whole story includes his high school and college disappointments. It includes his disappointments early in the NBA. You can focus on the success and his status as the best player ever. Yet his ability to overcome his failures is more instructive. His failures are what ignited the determination to improve, do better and ultimately become the greatest.

Rigidity from Perceived Failures

Rigidity is what causes many companies to fail. *"Who Moved My Cheese?"* is a book that I would recommend to anyone, young, old, or otherwise. I think of a company like Netflix in comparison with Blockbuster Video. Netflix filled the space from ordering DVDs from the comfort of your home to downloading them to your home device. They moved again to become a production company, cable network, and media streaming company all in one. They failed in multiple approaches, most famously attempting to raise their prices. Yet those failures were overcome. Meanwhile Blockbuster was slow to adopt new technology and business practices. I don't have much to say because the company is no longer in business.

Failing is connected to change and transformation. Rarely is a person able to change without a situation or series of occurrences that come into play. A failure, embarrassment, low point in life, or a storm precipitates that much needed propelling change. The situation causes you to think, "I cannot continue in this vein with these habits and have the freedom I need in my life." It is a specific feeling of failure in a specific area. It does not have to be like anyone else's experience. You could be making 6 figures in your firm and something causes a radical shift in your desire. You could in fact, have attained the peak of success in the eyes of others, but internally, feel deprived, stuck, constrained, and unhappy. It is not black or white. It is not up to outsiders to determine. These moments are what creates the need for change and transformation in your life.

I often take screenshots of supportive and motivational memes. As I was writing this chapter, I ran across a meme that showed a caterpillar sitting at the table talking to a butterfly. The caterpillar says, "You've changed."

"We're supposed to." The butterfly responds. We are supposed to evolve. YOU are supposed to evolve. It is the human experience. Learn about yourself and others. Learn more about human nature and how we interact. Often, we are worried about what another person thinks or how they are progressing in their lives: don't be stuck in this cycle, it is a waste of energy. Be mindful of using your energy towards situations that don't benefit you, don't add value but rather drain and transfer negativity. Normalize and embrace change as it is not only necessary, but also beneficial. Pay attention to your process and transformation rather than questioning another's. As women, it is especially important to applaud the growth of others. When one of our sisters is excelling, it is a win for all women no matter if it is your turn or not. It is not competition but rather a testament that it can be done and that you can be next. Instead of being envious, how about taking notes and celebrating?

Rosa sat so Ruby could walk so Kamala could run.

If we cheer other women and view the transformation process as normal, we gain a sense of humility, community, and trust. The achievement is not just for the woman succeeding. Vice President Kamala Harris famously stated that she has not achieved for herself alone.

"While I may be the first woman in this office, I will not be the last, because every little girl watching tonight sees that this is a country of possibilities." She recognizes how women before her inspired her to push forward, breakthrough, and succeed. Her torch was lit by someone, and she will continue to light the fire for others. When women unite, communities are elevated. Women contribute back to the community in multiple ways. We nurture. We influence households. We diversify boardrooms. We lead nations. We are truly unstoppable but we can't achieve this if we are rooting for another one of our sister's downfall in order for us to have a win. This isn't sisterhood. This is insecurity, and it is far from being okay! Look within and see if you have been trying to see another woman fail. Fix it! Let's operate in celebrating each other's wins even if our turn has not arrived *yet*.

"A glowing woman can help other women glow and still be lit." -Unknown.

You Might Win Some but You Just Lost One

Believe it or not, I'm up at 3 am with my husband watching Creed (the first one), for the first time. Keep in mind this portion was written in 2018, yes, it's now 2021...stop judging me!! The reason I am letting you know that is so that you can understand any times referenced or ages and stages of individuals included. Yes, this project has taken me about four or five years but the message is, I persisted. I continued. I hope you catch that! Okay back to Creed. The subtle and intentional messages of determination, validation, dreams, and pursuing passions are expressed throughout this film. Not only am I up late at night (or better yet early in the morning) watching this film, I am also becoming empowered. My husband and I are both working on pursuing our individual and collective goals and throwing ideas around about how we are beginning the process of going for our next, our greater goals.

When you hit the canvas, others think you're down for the count. YOU think that you're down for the count. BUT something ignites that fire to bring you back. To put you back in the game. The fight with Creed and Conway looks like it's over.

"I gotta prove it. Prove that I'm not a mistake." This is a statement Creed made regarding others' belief that he was just his father's shadow or legacy without putting the requisite work in. Creed landed a thunderous right hook dropping the greatest fighter in his generation to the canvas. Had the fight continued only a few more seconds, he would have been victorious. Creed did not win the fight, but he showed the ability to not only stay in the fight but potentially defeat anyone that stepped in the ring. He laid the framework for what would become a legendary career. Initially, he was fighting to win that title. He wanted to prove that he wasn't given the opportunity just because of who his father was but because he was truly worthy. At the end of the fight, the same opponent who told him he was nothing, unworthy, and didn't work to get to where he is, told him that he was the future. He realized that he had it in him to be a champion; that he had what it takes. It didn't take him winning to prove that he was capable, just as good, and worthy; it took him losing, fighting, and remaining in the game. We must realize that victory isn't always winning. In fact, many times, those that are considered the "winners" don't always shine compared to those that they competed against. When you feel discouraged, let this knowledge guide you.

Think about Skeleton Crew. Familiar with them? Me neither (no shade at all). In 1993, Skeleton Crew won Star Search, beating girl group "Girls Tyme" (later on becoming Destiny's Child). Had Girls Tyme won, what would have been the outcome of Destiny's Child or even Queen Bey? Would they have had to follow the guidelines and style of those on Star Search who signed them and been overlooked if their music wasn't a hit? Would it have limited their reach or impact? I am always impressed by the comeback of those who seemed to "lose" but were eventually victorious in a much bigger way, nonetheless. Watching Jennifer Hudson accept the Best Supporting Actress award for Dreamgirls just THREE YEARS after losing American Idol to then contestant Fantasia Barrino gave me such pride. I felt an overflow of joy for her win. What if *she* didn't realize her win in the loss? What if that 'L' was enough for her to not pursue her dream and fulfill her purpose? What dream are you sitting on? Have you let your temporary loss or setback deter you from birthing your purpose?

The worst thing you can ever do to yourself is allow your past or present loss to paralyze you or lead you to believe you are defeated. You must realize the power within YOU and the many who need your gift to make it, excel, and level up. Your voice is overdue. There are countless people suffering waiting to hear your voice, your message, experience your gift to the world. Release that fear, that doubt and heal from that point.

Take notes from it, move on, keep going. Stay in the race queen. In the words of my mentor and imaginary big sister, Lisa Nichols, "our gifts today were birthed from our failures of yesterday."

The Loss is a Win

Depending on how you choose to look at the experience, the loss can be a win. The most sustainable option is to level up in an area. Use the experience as a lesson. The "loss" was a necessary strategy for your win. As I read *Rich Dad, Poor Dad* I noticed the wisdom that could be applied to this pandemic. Too often, according to the author, we play life safe to the extreme in a way that cripples us when our environment experiences a lack of safety like losing your job. Our approach must be to approach choices as a steppingstone to create freedom for ourselves.

Everything is not always dualistic. I have two friends with opposite personalities. One is pessimistic while the other is optimistic. My pessimistic friend says often, "This is the reality." She states that she has tried "that positivity stuff" before as if it is a one-time practice that ends if it does not come with immediate results. Relationship or opportunity losses are just seen as "it is what it is." The reality keeps her from seeking what she passionately wants to accomplish. Pessimistic people often give up quickly in the face of discomfort and difficulty. They have experienced disappointment and loss. That is common to all, but those experiences support a narrative of despair and a curse of bad luck. You cancel out the effort when you promote the negative with your speech. You have the power to choose between speaking negativity or speaking destiny. Everyone gets lemons in life, even those we may see as 'perfect' and free from challenges. You could choose to look like you are sucking on lemons or you could make lemonade.

My optimistic friend on the other hand is always concerned about the energy that is present in a situation as well as her environment. She burns sage and cleanses her environment and her spirit. She is consistent with setting boundaries that protect her peace, her space, and enhance her growth. The benefits she enjoys are not the result of force and pursuit. They occur as the natural outcomes of her consistency and attention to kindness, connection, and reciprocity. She refuses to engage in the negativity that threatens to create emotional and mental suppression. Her life reflects what she practices, manages, and maintains. She has goals that stretch her in ways that she is happy to stretch rather than uncomfortable movements; it is intentional yoga.

Connection and attachment are the choices available to you. The Connection is like a power outlet. It is governed by a set of rules. Attachment is a leech. The leech sucks energy (blood) continually not considering the host. You have these choices, but it is more complex than that. You can draw a line down the middle of the paper and list the pros and cons of the experiences you have had. Reflect on what has been gained before dwelling upon what has been lost. What has been lost is gone. It sounds harsh, but the loss is irreconcilable, but peace of mind, sense of self, self-awareness outside of relationships, and more could have been gained. During the pandemic, think about what you may have gained in the midst of such great loss; did you gain perspective, clarity, freedom, time with family, time to work on building your business, time to just be, or other benefits? Reflect on those gains. Leverage them for additional gains. Look for the blessing in disguise. That is what I want you to reframe. Make a conscious decision to see the complexity in your experience and those moments that force you out of routine and into personal growth.

If you are one who is open to the idea and the search for silver linings within clouds, you can find something to celebrate or at least something to build upon. In my experience, I would not have looked at adjustments to my mortgage or other adjustments to my time usage. The pandemic gave me the motivation to complete my book after *years*, complete unfinished tasks in my home, launch my business and grow in my career. All could have been done prior to March 2020 however the push didn't feel as urgent. With the expectancy of this pandemic, I was reminded of the gift of time and the gift in my voice and of my purpose. I have walked in my purpose for over a decade; however, I am now running in my purpose! I am grateful for the wake-up call. For the push. The pandemic has been the worst experience for many, however with that being true, it has always been an opportunity to change. We made major changes within our home and finances because we were prompted by the feeling that we needed to create an environment for us to succeed even if things happen. The unexpected should always be expected. That is what the pandemic taught me. I am continuously reminded of the precious gift of life and intentionally living it in my gift. I desire the same for you sis. Walk in your gift unapologetically. Stop shrinking your gifts to accommodate or elevate others. You are needed, your gift is necessary, and others are waiting. Literally, right now! Don't deprive your tribe by neglecting your calling.

Think of at least three positive things you identified within the pandemic. Many of us struggle to identify any positive outcome of a calamity so let's work through it. Here are three that came to mind. The first one is obvious. You are reading this book. You are breathing. That means that you are living and have another opportunity to heal, grow, and walk in your freedom. Secondly, the fear of jumping is removed for you. I know this because this pandemic has shown you that anything can be taken away without warning. You either jump or are left behind. If you cannot change in the context of serious pressure, you will not change. Third, I encourage you to value the change itself as a positive thing. Be intentional about identifying the gains. It could be that you do not have the pressure to get up earlier in the morning. You may not have the commute again. Focus on the gain represented within your new reality.

"Not everything that is faced can be changed, but nothing can be changed if it is not faced." James Baldwin

You do not have complete control. But how you choose to express certain things, how you talk about your reality WILL make it so. When we spend more time thinking about our lack, we don't focus on the resources we *do* have and the ways that are made even in our loss or our lack. I have put in the consistent effort to speak life instead of struggle in my communication. It is not that I am blinded or disconnected to the reality that I am faced with, but rather intentional attention to the opportunities and strengths as well as the weaknesses and threats. You must speak the reality that you want to see. To begin speaking positively say what it is you desire; "My life will get better. This is a low point, but my high point is coming. I am coming out of this greater than I went in. What is intended for me, will be." You don't have to believe it when you say it, but when you repeat it, over and over, your mind becomes retrained. Speak*Believe*Do. This is my mantra. You will begin to see changes and recognize that jewels are added to your crown. Stating the affirmations consistently reminds ourselves of what is going to be; we begin believing it. Similar to the self-doubts we believe because we were told them over and over again and we believed them. We must oversaturate those negative beliefs with our desires through speaking it. Do you recall the Royal Horticulture Society study I mentioned in the previous chapter? The results were astounding but no different than what occurs with people. The negative talk (from others or ourselves) cause us to shrivel up, shrink, decline, and ultimately die (emotionally, spiritually or physically). Positive words however enhance your growth, they provide emotional and spiritual nourishment, cancelling out the doubts, limiting beliefs and even imposter syndrome (feelings as though you are not good enough). Speaking positivity can be stating positive affirmations posted around your home as reminders of who you are, using an app to share daily affirmations, guided meditation (I highly recommend Deepak Chopra's guided meditation), ASMR (autonomous sensory meridian response), prayer, or even a combination. Identify the path necessary to fulfill the desire help you to see that gains occur and exceed your expectations. Whatever the loss of income, relationships, or status, look for the returns pressed down, shaken together, and running over. Your beliefs won't manifest without the action. Growth is not just a process, it takes work. Let's get to work queen!

Reflection Questions

1. What losses have you experienced where you later experience gains?
2. What have you put off due to the fear of failing?
3. What challenges or failures have you learned from?

Chapter 4
Energy from Loss & Haters

What does a loss mean to you? According to Merriam-Webster's Dictionary, a loss is defined as a failure to gain, win, obtain, or utilize. Notice the word failure is included in the meaning. As the late and great Tupac Shakur said "...and if you fall, stand tall and come back for more." Falling doesn't equate failure and failure doesn't equate the end. I need that to settle in. Say aloud, "I am not a failure. My past mistakes don't dictate my future success. I am no longer a prisoner of my past. I have been freed from myself!" Release yourself from the cell that you've placed yourself in, sis. Freedom awaits you, however you must remember that you have the key. Unlock, release, unleash and walk into your newness. Free. Stop punishing yourself for the past; grow from it. Heal from it. Help other women by sharing your story which may help prevent them from going down a similar road; but also let them know that the wrong turn isn't the end. There is redemption, there is healing, there is freedom. Any queens reading this that are physically imprisoned right now, know that freedom goes beyond the physical. Becoming mentally and emotionally free is the freedom I speak of. This freedom is available to you sis. But it's impossible to gain freedom when we refuse to let go of the past. When we don't forgive ourselves or those that placed us in this emotional prison, we are doing ourselves a disservice and choosing to remain in a space we don't desire to be. Forgiveness is for you; it is freeing for you. It will hurt to relive the pain inflicted, the undeserved mistreatment but don't double your pain. The pain itself is more than enough but holding on to it causes you consistent heartache, pain, resentful, anger, and sadness all at once. One assignment I provided to a client who was a victim of abuse as a child was to write a letter to her deceased abuser. She said this was one of the most challenging tasks she was given and until beginning therapy, hadn't realize how much anger resided in her since she didn't talk about it. It showed up in other areas and towards other people although she didn't realize where it stemmed from. When she wrote the letter in between our weekly sessions, she shared with me how she felt a large amount of pressure released from her and that a weight was lifted off her. She cried as she read the letter (the first of three) that she had written to one abuser. She shared how she felt, the love she had for them, the pain she experienced from them, the moments of fear and humiliation and also the desire to no longer hold on to this pain anymore. She ended the letter with saying she forgave her abuser and that she just wished she had been able to do this before their passing. Hearing her speak regarding this situation and her journey of forgiveness was moving to say the least. For 50+ years, she had been burdened with these feelings of anger, rage, sadness, blame, doubt and fear due to no fault of her own. She didn't ask for nor deserve what happened to her. Releasing these feelings from her heart came in the form of forgiveness. She had to forgive not to allow them (even in death) off of the hook, but to free *herself.* If you are holding on to years of pain, resentment, anger from someone else's actions (abuse, cheating, lying, stealing, manipulating, racism, sexism, homophobia, the list goes on) you *owe* it to yourself to free yourself from that chronic anger and pain. The journey to freedom includes a pit stop at all the areas of our heart that aren't serving us and that need to be released. It's not your responsibility to hold on to it. The pain was enough. Don't burden yourself with continuing to hold on to the unwelcomed and undeserved pain sis. Forgive, as challenging as it may feel and be, it is not for them. It is for you. Be free queen, be free.

I truly believe that everyone needs a CORE of support. Every queen needs a court—a core of supporters. Each of you must bring this set of supportive realities to the relationship. This is the most sustainable experience for human beings but especially for women. Consistency, Openness, Reciprocity, Empathy; You must understand how to allow relationships to pass away without drama or a narrative of something terrible happening. Whether romantic or platonic, we often create a narrative that sets the other up as   evil. Even if there is nothing wrong, we often feel that some negative feeling needs to be applied to them for us to move on. Stop this. Everyone will not vibe with you, neither will everyone be a part of your tribe and that's okay. The cost is too high. It costs your peace. I have taken the Nipsey Hussle quote to heart:

"If you cost me my peace, you have to go."

Rather than introduce haters as evil, I want to present to you that haters are just former or potential relationships that are not serving you AND they have created a narrative of negativity. Regardless of what the other person did or didn't do, continue to grow and move forward. People will remove themselves. There is no maliciousness or negative intent to be explained. Growth creates its environment for health, wellbeing, and longevity.

Birthing Something New

Many times, our shortcomings are what births something new. This reminds me much of the life of a caterpillar. Very slow, stubby, and in my opinion unattractive insect whose life expectancy in that state, as a caterpillar, is relatively short. The only purpose it serves is to build a cocoon (chrysalis). During this "grooming" process, the caterpillar does nothing else but prepare for the next. The process may seem boring, tedious and at times unnecessary. Guess what? It's also somewhat messy, just like our own growth process. But after that preparation for a greater purpose is complete, the caterpillar can release itself and birth something greater. The grooming process was preparing that slow, stubby caterpillar to transform into a beautiful, colorful, smooth butterfly that now has the ability to soar, seeing the world in a whole new light from a completely different view. Genuine friendship is important to show up as your authentic self. You know when a friend needs your support because they are different than they are normal. If the need is the norm, you may need to assess who is in your tribe and if you are adding to each other or if only one is adding while the other is always the recipient, sucking life continuously out of the partnership. Connection over attachment. Remember when I mentioned the leech? Assess your tribe ladies.

"Watching a performance can be exhausting. It's refreshing to spend time with those who are free enough to show up as their authentic selves." Dr. Thema Bryant

Consistency. Consistency looks like a pattern and trend. If you have someone who is always in need of money, you can at least say that they are consistent. Whether positive or negative, consistency builds trust and an expectation. For my circle, queens consistently show up for me as I, for them.

Openness. Reintroduction of yourself as you grow requires others to respect that growth. If you have owned, learned and grown from an experience, your circle supports that. Refuse to put the weight of your friend's existence on yourself. Do not allow your friends to take on too much of your weight. The way to balance this is not Science or Math. It will not be 38% for each person tallied in a log. It is an art that is responsive to life and its variability. The only way to effectively balance this, is by proper communication.   Check-in with your circle. See how the balance feels and is experienced. If you feel like you are the only one doing the pouring, check in with your tribe. Communicate. If it isn't serving you, feel free to communicate that and if you desire, align yourself with a tribe that is more suitable to your needs and what you can provide as well. Disconnection does not equate to shade or hate. You just may not be matched in the new or current season that you're in and that is okay.

Reciprocity. I saw a meme that stated, "I no longer pour into cups that do not pour into mine." It spoke to me. It is a reminder that I must maintain a level of substance if I am going to contribute my best to others. I refuse to deplete myself. Healthy relationships are built in the balance. I have been guilty of providing too much without requiring reciprocity in return. The return does not need to be the same contribution. It only needs to be consistent, valuable to both parties and communicated if possible. Balance is supported by appropriate boundaries. Set them for yourself and others. Stick to them.

Empathy. When I am telling you something, first feel and respond to where I am coming from. Put yourself in my shoes and see how I am seeing it. A good friend will always tell you the truth and let you know what you did wrong, if anything, or how you can improve. But, it is critical to listen closely to a friend and hold their feelings and perspective with understanding. Regardless of what occurred, their feelings are valid, as are yours.

When Lightning Strikes

Storms do not only destroy, they clear paths as well. Learn to see the storm not just for all that it takes away and limits, but also what it provides and makes possible. Failure is an idea that we are introduced to very early on in life, however it's important to realize that there is a vast difference between fail*ure* and fail*ing.* Failing is a weakness or a shortcoming. A failure is an unsuccessful person. Some synonyms for failing are deficiency, weakness, and imperfection. Failure on the other hand is synonymous with non-fulfillment, loser, and defeat. Have you ever seen the movie Cars? If not, you are truly missing out. I watched the movie years ago but watching it this year especially while I'm in transition into my next (yes, I too am always growing), it hit differently. There is one car in particular whose character is very profound, more so than the main character Lightning McQueen in my opinion. The car named Doc Hudson is known to the other cars as an upstanding 'citizen' and well known in the community as a former resident doctor and a judge. He is always helping others and they glean to him for wisdom. Although they view him as someone with a lot of knowledge, they repeatedly failed to see the depth of his greatness due to his appearance; he's an older car and doesn't ride around in a braggadocious manner as the other racing cars do. Think about him as being maybe a 70-year-old retiree. One day while Lightning McQueen was stuck in Radiator Springs (a town he is not too familiar with) he begins speaking with other cars and talks with Doc Hudson for a little bit. After leaving Doc, he drives off and notices an off-limits area. How did he know it was off-limits you ask? Because it was marked by Doc himself. McQueen decides to poke his head into the off-limit area at Doc's garage and to his surprise, finds trophies, pictures, and articles about the Fabulous Hudson Hornet who had won the most prestigious racing awards in history. Picture talking to your local barber M.J. and coming across his private room which housed his 6 rings, Chicago Bulls jersey, and pictures of M. J. but with Michael Jordan written all over it.   Mind-blowing right? THAT's how major this was. This small-town car being a former superstar in the same field that McQueen was currently the star in was unbelievable.

How could no one know? Did they not see his gift? How is it that greatness was in front of everyone the entire time, but it was overlooked? While McQueen is admiring all of the awards and in awe, Doc pulls up slowly behind him, very upset and asking him about why he entered if he read the signs. McQueen left and received no answers to his inquiries. McQueen goes back to his 'crew' and tells them that Doc is really the Fabulous Hudson Hornet. Their response was laughter and downplaying referring to him as old, and not equipped with the ability to win championships. He's just an old car. Doc hears these responses from the crowd of cars, and you know what? Those doubts and humiliation from others validated his feelings of void, worthlessness, and unfulfillment. They viewed him now as a nobody, not even a "has-been." They did not and could not believe that HE could have actually been the Fabulous Hudson Hornet. Who would throw that gift away? Who wouldn't flaunt who they were or even assist others in becoming the next or even better version?

Reframing the Hate

Later on, in the movie, Lightning McQueen sees Doc and he is cleaned up and revving up his engine. He begins racing solo, just seeing if he still had it. You know what? He *did*. That gift that was his, didn't leave. It never leaves because it's his-and your gifts are yours! It can't be stolen. He believed he was no longer capable because others said he wasn't. He fulfilled THEIR prophecy. But what about his, over his own life? His purpose? At this point, McQueen is in disbelief because now he not only saw the receipts of who he was, but he now sees it in action. Unable to fully process all that he had just witnessed, he asked Doc "How could a car like you quit on the game?" Doc looks back and responds almost in disgust "You think I *quit*?" He explains to McQueen that when he came back from the crash, he was told his career was over. That he was done. The tragic part was not that he crashed or the makeup repair being faulty, but that he believed the doubters. He had been in his town around his friends for years and nobody knew his story, his value, what he was, who he was. His gift was silenced, and his light was dimmed, but not extinguished. If you go up a few lines and reread, you will find the answer to my next question. What propelled him to remember who he was and what value he had? Many times, in life we are bothered by the whispers of the naysayers and the haters but when I began to reframe my thinking, I became truly grateful for them. Sometimes the only thing that can push and propel us into greater are our haters. Many times, they are our biggest fans, they just haven't received the memo yet. You can choose to become bitter by the hate or better because of it. The crew who laughed at the gas station when McQueen informed them of who Doc was did nothing but refuel Doc's passion. His initial feeling of sadness and worthlessness arose which then became frustration, boiled into anger, and manifested into determination. He became determined to not only prove himself to others but to prove himself to himself. What are you letting your haters do for you? Word to the wise, they are not going anywhere-I can guarantee you they, whoever the 'they' are in your life, are not going anywhere for the duration of your life. I advise you to use the gift of "hateration" for your benefit. Doing otherwise only holds you up and fulfills their prophecy over YOUR life. No, that doesn't serve you at all. Instead, let them work for you, for FREE by reminding you of your gift or even that you won't succeed! Use that as fuel, queen. Remember that this or any other low point in your life isn't the book of your life. It may not even be a full chapter but rather a page in your book of life. I will share one of the most profound phrases with you that comes from a song I loved when I was in college. It's very simple to remember. *Big ups to all my haters!* I thank you all but I do apologize as there are too many to name, but I'm grateful for the push! My cousin says, "What they admire in you is what they lack in themselves. That's why they hate. Keep on shining." That is my hope for you. Shine on queen and don't allow the naysaying to paralyze your growth but rather, allow it to charge you up and level up.

Reflection Questions

1. What are your definitions of consistency, openness, reciprocity, and empathy?
2. How have you applied those definitions in your relationships?
3. How do you speak consistency, openness, reciprocity, and empathy in your daily communications?

Chapter 5
Adjusting and Shifting

"When someone falls in love with your flower, not your root, they don't know what to do when fall and winter comes." -Jade Jackson

When people see you without the flower, the makeup, or the covering of social grace, they may not be able to maintain their comfort. When they see you for who you are in your rawness and pain, they may not be able to support you. That you without the mask is critical to reveal to yourself so that you may begin to heal. Heal for healthy relationships. Become a victor, rather than a victim. Victims survive but victors thrive and share their victory to empower others. How are you choosing to overcome?

Victor Rather than Victim

Success isn't specific to numbers. Success is being at peace within. Peace within is the prerequisite to exuding peace externally—a peace that cannot be shaken. I can't determine what peace is for you, however when you achieve the awareness of what your definition of peace is, and achieve that, you find success. Everything becomes secondary and "easier" in a way.

You will then gain the ability to focus on what truly matters, your innermost desires.

Beyond energy, the outward and inward attention and awareness become an intentional construction of your environment. Your environment, including what you put in your space, your body, and your mind, is crucial to your peace, productivity, and success. For example, while you may not be a "neat freak" who is always bothered by the environment being clean and tidy, the intention you give to your environment feeds your spirit. I challenge you to be consistent with the process. You may not be tidy but choose to hire a cleaning service because you realize that a tidy space is crucial to the experience of a peaceful environment.

Brokenness, damage, and lack of forgiveness are the clutter that robs us of peace. You are likely to hurt others as a result of unresolved pain and trauma, similar to how other hurting individuals have hurt you. Acceptance, compassion, and empathy are the emotional attendants of peace. Your job is to make intentional choices about what you want, do not want, will tolerate, and will refuse to support these emotions. The first action toward cultivation is your speech.

Victims talk about what they went through. The transition to change does not occur. Victors speak of moving beyond the now toward a greater level of knowledge and success as you see it. If we have a victim mentality, we continue to cage ourselves and keep ourselves from expanding and exploring. If you use the occurrences as a motivator to learn and grow, your experience becomes a steppingstone. Many activists, nonprofit founders, and community leaders respond to experiences that threatened to take life from them. They turn the situation around to make a difference in their communities. Often times birthing purpose from their pain and testimony from their trauma.

I have seen so many examples of this throughout my life. A family friend lost her son to gun violence over 15 years ago. She founded a nonprofit and provides healing to her community through violence prevention workshops, block parties, food drives, and giveaways. The benefit of the community is not just a story of tragedy, but an everlasting impression of triumph through pain. Tiffany Haddish began her organization, She Ready Foundation, to ensure that children in foster care have a suitcase to hold their belongings rather than trash bags. She birthed this from a place of pain and trauma she experienced as a foster child moving from one place to the next, forced to toss her belongings in trash bags. She decided that because of, not despite, her experience as a victim, she would serve. "Because of" not "despite" because the lack of weakness motivates the search for greater and the action for change.

Mentality, growth, and perspective are what the victor gains. Mentality shifts from feeling sorry for yourself dwelling in that sorrow and defining your future opportunity based on that experience, to taking your power back. Work through what has occurred with a victor mentality. Forgive to free yourself; it's for you, not for them. We sometimes think we are punishing "them" by holding on to the harm done, but we are only punishing ourselves. The long-term detriment is undeniable.

Growth recognizes that each experience, good and bad, are bricks in the foundation of our lives. Growth is achieved when the "Why me?" becomes the "Now, What?" You grow into a purpose motivated by your experience, informed by your search for answers and development beyond the experience. Marvin Sapp's song comes to mind: *"Thank you For It All"*. He sings about being thankful for all that he endured including the good, bad, ugly, victorious times and times that he stumbled. I recommend you take a listen- copyright infringement is real so I won't share the lyrics but the song is powerful.

Perspective can be the empathetic lens through which you understand and help others who are in that situation. Perspective allows you to identify the pain point from multiple perspectives, resulting in empathy. In 2019, America watched as Botham Jean's brother hugged and forgave his brother's killer. Many did not understand how he could give so much to someone who had taken so much away from his family. Perspective allows us to understand that he needed that to heal himself. He moved from being a victim to a victor. The perpetrator does not become a saint that did nothing wrong, but the victor takes responsibility for their own healing. Remember, forgiveness is for you-it's imperative in your journey to healing and freedom. The perpetrator can be seen as human, still the antagonist and guilty, but human - nevertheless releasing their hurt, pain, and anger. You can recognize that you must refuse to hold hurt, pain, and anger and hurt others maintaining the vicious cycle of violence, abuse, and mistreatment. Release sis, release.

Looking Honestly in the Mirror

Chadwick Boseman's character in Ma Rainey's Black Bottom (set in the 1920s) responds to being teased for his response to a white man in a situation. He told the story of his prior encounter with white men in his childhood who caused harm (trying to avoid sharing specific details in case you haven't seen this phenomenal film). He buys a new pair of shoes at the beginning of the movie and near the end of the movie, someone stepped on his shoes. He is frustrated from the feelings he was forced to hold in with the white man, and he displaces that anger towards an older black man who accidentally stepped on his shoes; since this man was closer to him (in proximity), he became the easier target to unleash his pain and anger. His pain points were triggered, and he exploded on the person closest to him. You could see in his eyes, "This is all I had, and you took it away from me. Something else that was *mine*, taken from me." The sentiment was directed toward the older black man, but the energy was due to the treatment at the hand of the white man. Has this been you before? Have you felt overlooked and ignored, having your pain invalidated leading to hurting those closest to you? Or have you been the recipient of someone else's pain and anger due to you close proximity to them?

This illustrates the importance of knowing your triggers and processing them. You may not be triggered when looking into the mirror. You may have trouble seeing what is looking back at you. Sometimes, authenticity requires you to reflect on a situation you handled poorly. Sit and think without the emotions of the experience. Remove yourself. Take several deep breaths and ask yourself what was said. What truly happened without the translation of what you heard, their intentions, and how it made you feel?

I highly recommend that you process the experience to explore the feelings that arose for you, preferably with a therapist, a support group or at least with an unbiased party. Reflect on the situations, individuals, and emotions you felt in the experiences that fostered your feelings of inadequacy, insecurity, and vulnerability. Refuse the opportunity to defend yourself from attack. It is easy and feels completely justified to react to the pain that you feel. Often, you are addressing the pain with the dialogue that you have created as a result of the pain you felt unintentionally. You may have grown to defend yourself as a survival tactic—a way to return to safety in the context of feeling attacked. Defensiveness however limits our growth and ability to see ourselves, flaws and all.

The same energy that created the response to the trigger can be used to create an *appropriate* response to the trigger. It takes a great amount of energy to presume another person's intentions and translate what they said into a negative intention. What others think about you is not your business. Don't make it your business. That is their thought process and usually a projection of their own negative view of self. Their words may be extending from their own pain. When what they think does not matter, your goal is not to control or question their why. That energy could be used to control and question your why. Your identification and refusal to self-destruct allow you to create a new mentality, growth, and perspective in your life. We have the power to choose where and what we give our energy to; it can be used towards our empowerment and betterment or our detriment. Choose wisely.

Vulnerability

Initially, this is where I would have ended this chapter. I felt that it was somewhat dope, real and helpful but one thing that it is missing is vulnerability. One of my closest friends since kindergarten, Brittney, loved where I was going but said, "girl this is amazing and it's on point but how much of you are you going to share? How vulnerable are you willing to be?" Whew child...this was a stretch that was necessary.

She is definitely one of my sounding boards. We stayed up until 3 am that night talking about our different challenges and how growing up we have both always internalized our feelings and blocked our vulnerable side. After hearing her suggestion, I knew she was right...so I will open up, get naked, and share pieces of my walk in order to help you with your growth. I hope that if you identify with parts of me, that you will be able to better self-reflect and work through your luggage, both past, and present.

You may not become the perpetrator in the same manner that it was perpetrated on you, but unresolved pain will become rage that is visited upon those nearby. Many become what they despise or what hurt them. They are trained in that abuse, and that becomes the default in their defense of self. The cycle must be broken, and a new set of responses introduced. Repeat or Repel. You must repel intentionally.

I have examples from my early growth experience while blowing up on my husband. I unleashed misdirected pain upon him at times. I knew I could. I felt that he was a safe option for my release. No, it wasn't fair or deserving, but it was my reality. Many of us feel that some people are ride or die. We test it and prove their loyalty by acting out with them as the recipient. My husband would notice my emotion in the space and remind me that it was not his failure or fault that put me in my feelings. I realized that my trigger was in response to a feeling of shrinking in the context of a man based on several examples provided by various women I admired and looked up to from childhood to adulthood. I witnessed many women neglect and starve their desires to further the goals and desires of their significant other. I perceived this as shrinking to accommodate a man. I did not want to be a woman that shrank in order to make a man, or anyone, comfortable or validated. Over the years, I took a moment to understand the influence many of these women had from the older women in their lives including mothers, aunts, and grandmothers and their upbringing. Understanding who they wanted to be, and what brought them joy to recognize how these choices of putting their spouses' desires and needs before their own made sense for them. I was fighting against this in my own relationship while it had never been my fight, nor my story all along! This is powerful, because we sometimes internalize the battles of those whose lives we've closely mirrored, and then proceed to fight non-existent battles in our own lives.

I remember a situation where I was going to pick up one of my little cousins (a child) late at night in a not-so-great area. My husband suggested that it may be better to go in the morning and we would both go. I became very defensive and felt like he was telling me what to do. I was not having it. I hopped out of the car in icy conditions. I stormed off...in four-inch knee high boots in an unfamiliar area. *"What are you doing? I made a suggestion trying to look out for you because I care and want you safe. That's it."* He kept asking me to get back in the car and to calm down as I walked in the cold on an icy street in the middle of the night. Like I was tripping for real for real. I felt that I had to prove a point and make sure that others knew the type of woman that I am. Anything that was correcting or telling a woman what to do, I addressed through my perception of malicious intent. It took a while for me to cool down, probably aided by the fact that it was so cold outside. I grew to understand the difference between loving care and the controlling of a woman. I can now be the best of myself without shrinking to be other roles like mother, wife, employee, or other. I can just be. You can too. Don't be less of who you are because of your additional titles and roles in the lives of others. Don't allow examples of toxicity to spill into your reality. You can be an awesome mom, wife, girlfriend, employer, employee, sister, and more while not once shrinking yourself to accommodate the needs or desires of others.

But allow me to reintroduce myself! I am no longer that woman hopping out of cars to prove a point or being defensive to ensure I am not viewed or portrayed a certain way. Never allow others to define you based on your past but rather continue to grow from your past and realize it was all part of your journey and an essential part of *your* story.

Reflection Questions

1. In what areas of your life have you released your anger or hurt onto others who were not the perpetrators?
2. What triggers do you recognize within yourself?
3. How do you work through those triggers to inform, reconstruct, and heal them?

Section II

The Process

Chapter 6
Reintroducing You: Changing the Narrative

Let us separate the false and problematic reality of pretentiousness from the new definition of self that I am promoting. Refuse what others may find for themselves in definitions tied to the treatment, expectations, or desires of others. Develop a definition that extends from your evaluation of self. The transformation could require answering to a new name, but the results are to see yourself in a new light. You may need to ask for help and accept that relationships can have reciprocity. One thing is for certain, you will CHANGE.

Your New Name

Had your story not occurred, you would not be shaped into who you are. You are a piece of a puzzle. You have been shaped to fit by what you have been through. What you went through impacts the person you are and what you have worked to become is part of the story. You are your "becoming person."

To whom this may concern: Delete that old version of you in your head. It expired. Few people will give you credit or acknowledge your growth on your path to becoming. That's okay-it's none of your business what they think or how they view you. They are comfortable with the old you. Often times your growth exposes them. It causes them to look in the mirror if they have not done the work themselves. Don't let that deter you! Strangers may even recognize your presence and have trouble accepting that you were different in a prior encounter. The difference is that they are rarely intimidated by your growth, unlike someone who's always known you. However, be it a stranger or an insider, be ready to remind people through your behavior to experience you in the present. Own your triggers and your past explosions or poor behavior.

At this moment, you must exhibit a certain level of selfishness or rather selflessness with yourself. Again, not selfishness as stingy, but selfishness with regards to prioritizing self-care, self-assessment, freedom to process self and personal perspective first. Your soul work must be primary. Your heart work must be at the center of your reintroduction.

Apologize for what you may have done, but never apologize for your growth. Anyone who refuses to see you for the new person you're becoming is the one who needs to evolve. Don't ever feel guilty for requesting proper treatment. You may make a formal apology to the people you have hurt. You may disregard your childhood nicknames and insist upon your given name. One of my clients actually goes by her middle name only, so as to no longer be connected or identified as the person she used to be. Many years back, there was a church elder who we affectionately referred to as Uncle Butch. He gave a testimony one day where he talked about his change and the development from Butch to his given name of Alex. It was a difficult transition for many in the church as we were used to a certain name, but that is the explicit reality that expresses the symbol of his change. It is not easy especially for others who are used to seeing you a certain way, but if they respect you, then they'd acknowledge your new reality. Walk into your newness, with your new shoes, and if necessary a new name, daily. As people see that, they become accustomed to speaking of you as a new person with a new name. Don't be fearful of outgrowing the former you for the better version of you. Change is uncomfortable but transformation is fulfilling.

Adjusting

One of the most challenging tasks I have found as I began to self-improve, define myself, my purpose, and level up is reaching out to others for assistance. What does that look like? When I refer to assistance, I'm talking about reaching out to those that can hold you accountable for your success, those that are providing you with wisdom and the tools to successfully establish and meet the goals we have set out for ourselves. I'd like to call these individuals sounding boards. As someone who doesn't like to ask for anything and when I say anything, I mean I'm extra with it. For example, if we're at a vending machine and debit cards aren't accepted (I rarely have cash on me), I would most likely not even ask you if I could borrow a dollar. If I *did*, please believe that by the time you handed me the dollar, your phone would chime because I would have already sent you the money in Cash App. That's how I've operated my entire life so I'm sure you could imagine how challenging it was to reach out to those who are now my sounding boards and ask for guidance, critiques, and even explain to them my vision. Talk about being out of my comfort zone. I realized that although I wanted to continue moving forward in my career and my self-actualization, I felt as though I was peaking. I was unable to further my growth without changing my diet, figuratively. I needed to be fed from others with more nutritious feasts and not just engaging with those with takeout meals. Now, we all can have a little takeout every so often-it fills us quickly when we need it and temporarily hits the spot, but long term it won't sustain us. It won't enhance us. Who is your sounding board? What table are you feasting from or are you only feeding off of takeout? To grow, it is critical to learn to be comfortable with being uncomfortable. I share this with not only my clients but to my students, my friends, and Lord knows I'm working on helping my family with this but sometimes wearing two hats causes a conflict. Conflict of interest. You know what I mean, don't you?

Refusal to seek help is common among women. We have been taught to *be* the helping hand. We are taught that we, alone, must make it happen. We are taught to be fully selfless and independent. Much of this is tied to fears of being left by a significant other who removes his or her support or a supporter who holds their support over our heads. As a result, women lift entire communities seldom having what they need to stay above water in their personal, relational, financial, and spiritual lives all at once. Trauma response. As women we worry that if we accept help, our motives may be questioned. We seek to conform to what others think. Often, we don't know what we think or desire outside of what others promote for us. The mask. Whew.

How willing are you to be uncomfortable? Is there a time limit to your discomfort? To move differently you have to act differently which involves self-reflection, self-assessment, changing your surroundings, and changing your mindset. If all of these remain the same, your dreams will remain dreams, your goals will remain unclear, and your purpose will remain unidentified and unfulfilled.

Back to the Rich Dad Poor Dad discussion: When the friends asked about how to become successful, the rich dad spoke about how people sought him for jobs, but they never asked about how to be successful. They did not ask about financial literacy or making your money work for you. He offered to teach the two young boys life lessons, not just providing them a small wage. He put him in a situation that was uncomfortable at the moment to set him up for a lifetime. He taught them to fish rather than just giving them the fish. The question was, "How bad do you want the learning?" Most, he suggests, only want the benefits of the moment rather than the lessons for a lifetime. You can say it is not fair and that you are missing too much, or you can get what it takes to propel and sustain you into the future. The choice is yours.

Too often, we bow to the needs of others rather than exploring what we want. It could be our parents who guilt us into thinking that their aspirations for us are our desires. It could be spouses that we desire to please and lose ourselves in the process. It could be kids that we feel obligated to accommodate to set them up for success. The challenge is the silence that results within us—the inability to know ourselves. Who are you beneath the mask, beneath the titles?

Shifting

The shift is going to be uncomfortable and different. It is also going to be worth it. It will be freeing. I've stated this several times throughout the book because the reminder is necessary. It's not a walk in the park. Think about the ways that you learned about the needs, wants, and patterns of your parents, husband, and children. It probably was not a list that they handed to you. It was time that you spent with them. They have been vocal about their needs and wants. You have taken the time to observe their patterns, triggers, and comfort zone.

You must sit with that same process for yourself. Refuse the tendency to say things like "I enjoy making my family happy." You may take joy in that. But what about your contribution gives you joy? What reactions and interactions are healing and feeding for you? You can maintain your connection with all those influencers. It makes sense to inform them of your needs, wants, and patterns. What you need and desire from them. Reciprocity. Your contributions must be reciprocated. Not only is it fair but you are deserving of it, sis. If you are giving out from your cup without receiving anything in return, you will be depleted. Live. Don't just exist. Living requires reciprocity. Reciprocity requires that you know what feeds you.

You don't realize how stuck you are when you are attempting to maintain a façade and an existence that seeks to please others. Some of us may not even know *how* reciprocity is supposed to feel. This discussion of freedom and reciprocity may feel and be foreign to you. You may accept that role of selflessness, sacrifice, and servitude. I am here to tell you that you can be selfless, independent, and serve with reciprocity and a clear vision of self. Shifting is a change. It will be a welcomed change. The completeness with any person is a bonus, a tax, an extra. You must be whole outside of any person and their expectation or perception of you. Their opinion must never take over *your* definition of self.

CHANGE Acronym

C-check your prescription. Evaluate yourself. How have you seen things from your perspective? Is your view distorted or one sided? What SMART goals are you setting and how will you obtain them? Smart goals are specific, measurable, attainable, relevant, and time-based. Identifying them is for evaluation of them and their contributions, but also of their influence. Create goals that solely benefit you and your desires. This may be a challenge for many, especially if your only identity has been through the existence of someone else i.e. child/ren, spouse, employment, parents, siblings. You must define yourself and your desires and identify what makes you happy. What fills you emotionally, mentally, spiritually and physically?

H-honor your commitment to grow. It is important that you remain committed to yourself in your journey to freedom. It may feel easier at moments to put more of your energy into enhancing and impacting the lives of others over your own, but in reality, you become *better* not just for you but for those you are connected to (spouse, child/ren, colleagues, friends, family).

A-adjust your mindset and get out of your comfort zone. This is challenging for everyone. We do what we do because we believe that it's right. We have to get out of our own way and outside of our former way of thinking to change our way of being. A fixed mindset will inhibit us from progressing and stunt our growth. Grow beyond the former limits you may have once placed on yourself. Be free my dear.

N-nourish yourself. Mind, body, soul. Read self-help/empowerment books. I suggest that everyone read the books: *"Mindset"* by Carolyn Dweck, *"The Four Agreements"* by Miguel Ruiz, *"No Matter What"* by Lisa Nichols, *"Who Moved My Cheese?"* by Dr. Spencer Johnson and *"Giving to Yourself First"* by Iyanla Vanzant, just to name a few. A balanced diet includes feeding your mind with tools that will not only empower you but assist you with the application and making the shift. Your mental health requires it. Whatever we nourish or starve our minds with, comes out in how we speak, engage and connect with others. It can show up in our mannerisms, our thought process, our defensiveness, our positivity, verbiage, and most importantly our way of thinking including the ability or inability to grow and shift. Nourish yourself, mind, body, spirit.

G-guidance. Who mentors you? Who holds you accountable for your growth and for putting yourself first? True growth requires accountability, guidance and mentorship. If you recall, I referred to these individuals as my sounding board. Our mindset at times is programmed to believe that our mentor must be someone that is more advanced than us in our particular field or make more money to gain quality mentorship which is too far from the truth to detail. President Barack Obama was counseled and mentored by Reverend Jeremiah Wright, Michael Jordan was mentored by Clifton Herring (HS), Dean Smith (college), and Phil Jackson (NBA), and Wynn Handman-the acting coach of Oscar recipients Denzel Washington and Robert DeNiro, who taught into his 90s until his recent passing in 2020. I want to also include Sonya Carson who taught her son Ben Carson to have a passion for learning, giving him book reports to complete at home while she "checked" his work although she herself couldn't read. He had no idea!!! Your mentor's success doesn't need to match yours, their gifting just needs to be impactful, consistent and pure. They communicate the strategy to enhance the area we are being mentored in.

E-evolve. Once you apply the other areas, you can then begin to evolve. You transform from the old to the new. You have been engaged in a process. Now, you are in the action phase of the change. This is the work of maintaining. Evolution is a daily routine with periodic evaluation of progress, momentum, and direction. Your life your choice. Doing the hard work is not enough. Kobe Bryant's guidance counselor told him he shouldn't play basketball and that it wouldn't amount to anything. All that did was make him stronger, pushing him to prove him wrong. You can't stop others from trying to limit your dreams, but you can stop their opinions and comments from becoming your reality. In the words of Sarah Jakes Roberts, *"Woman, evolve!"* We weren't born to be stuck, shrink, or simple. We are dynamic, powerful, forever evolving beings.

Reflection Questions

1. How are you making opportunities out of obstacles or are you making obstacles from presented opportunities?
2. Can you identify individuals you can collaborate with as mentors, sounding boards or accountability partners?
3. Describe what patterns, triggers, and comfort zone define you and influence your desires and what brings you joy.

Chapter 7
Free Your Mind: Mindset Shift

Your mind is the source of your being. You learned in school that a physical connection exists between your bodily functions and the control center of the brain. You may not have learned the emotional connections like fight, flight or freeze that are provided by your brain. Mental illness and emotional issues are stored in the brain. Certain experiences should limit your functioning, but your brain can compartmentalize experiences so that you can still function even through immense pain. Your mind files away or suppresses pain that can be triggered consciously or unconsciously.

Everything you want to do is triggered by the mind. If you want to lose weight, you cannot continue to complain and practice even the words of your failure. "I just can't stop eating cakes." If you say that you can't, you won't. When you put words into the atmosphere, it is as good as done, although not immediate. This is the law of attraction. Stop speaking negativity in your life even when you are joking. Your spirit, your mind does not know the difference. Your words speak power into your existence. When you speak, your mind activates based on those words. You champion the energy that you speak. Beliefs become actions. Actions show the thought process. Words draw the experiences toward you.

Begin to rehearse what you desire. You may not believe it in the beginning, but your words will train your mind AND attract your experience. Your words signal intention. Your intention prescribes action. Action creates reality. People recite "No weapon formed against me will prosper" yet we fail to realize at times we are the weapon formed against ourselves. You may not realize the negativity you form against yourself and your goals.

Silencing the Noise

The brain is trained. If you have experienced the trauma of emotional abuse, you may have a pattern of speaking negatively to yourself. Silencing that noise requires that you speak truth to that power. Recognize that the experiences you have had and the path you walked is not a confirmation of your purpose and future. They are the expression of the energy that you rehearsed and had thrust upon you. If the people you grow up around give you information, you are going to believe it. They provide what was provided to them.

Negativity will echo in your mind. You must speak the opposite in every instance. When your mind reminds you, "You will not amount to anything." Respond with, "I am powerful and can accomplish anything I want to do." These are positive affirmations. Continue consistently to counteract the negativity with multiple affirmations. Oversaturate the negative thoughts and beliefs with repetition. The positive will become second nature, just as the negative did.

You will cease to tolerate when people interact with you as if you are less than. You demand and command respect. You become more comfortable in environments that are healing rather than those that are toxic. Move within this experience of growth and freedom. Refuse the pressure to remain in the same relationship structures that damaged you. For example, every time you go around your childhood home, you may have those that treat you as a child who must "stay in your place." You may feel pressure to remain in these relationships, especially when the offenders are family. But family members are humans too. Just as you would change your friend's list to support your health, you must have the courage to organize your family connection list to support the same. You may not be able to attend every family function if you prioritize your mental health. You can't change anyone else, but you can improve yourself and remove yourself. Whoever it is that brings you into that dark space should no longer have limited access to your you; your wellbeing depends on it. Any family, platonic, or romantic entanglement that is toxic must be assessed and addressed to determine the impact on your emotional, mental, spiritual and physical wellbeing. No exceptions. Do not accept less than what you deserve because of who the person is, their position, status, relation, or otherwise. Toxicity is toxicity whether even if it's dressed up as and normalized as love.

Remove the drama and push to get momentum. Your past is your foundation no matter how terrible or beautiful. No matter how awful, you can overcome. No matter how beautiful it is only dressing for your next opportunity.

My husband and I were at a park last year teaching our son how to ride a two-wheeler. My son was fearful of us letting go so that he wouldn't fall. He had seen his peers ride successfully but was still afraid. My husband explained the process with words that I noticed were affirmations for us all. He stated that when pushing off to begin the bike ride, you must focus on what is ahead of you and the balance while riding. He said to my son "You push off so you can get momentum. If you look back, you will swerve off track and possibly fall."

This is wisdom for us as well. You can look back to see how far you have come but allowing the same environments and interactions can sabotage your progress. Just like a person who is recovering from alcohol dependency must guard their influences, we must guard our minds and what our environments and interactions suggest. Often times God is pushing us all to give us momentum. That is how I conceptualize the energy that is all around us. All we need to do is keep it going. He's prepared us for this. Are you ready to fly? Are you ready to soar? We can't tailor-make or design our type of push, our type of kickoff, that's already established, but we need to know that the only way to get momentum and into a rhythm is to push off and not to look back.

It's okay if you're falling. That's a part of the experience-learn and grow from it. The issue isn't in the fall. Failure is in not recovering from it. Not getting back up. Fall 7 times get up 8. You are responsible for your breakthrough. The energy you cultivate becomes the mind you nurture. Others can help you get to the wall of greatness, the wall of your destiny, but you and only you must be the one to break it down and burst through. Sis, you ready?

Identify Your Why

A sustainable mindset requires a clear reason for your action and purpose. I refer to this as 'Your Why.' Your purpose or Your Why is the reason you continue. It may be service to humanity, a sense of responsibility to your child or honoring a person who believed in you. This exercise is about unraveling the You. It is healing that leads to growth and freedom.

So, why do you need healing? Whatever it is that you can explain about your current experience, patterns would emerge to explain your experience. Everyone needs healing. Healing is a term that explains a process where you come to terms with your story and begin to value what you have gone through. Healing is the release of the negative feelings including anger and resentment surrounding painful experiences throughout our journey. You recognize the influences, triggers, and definitions that you have constructed to feel safe and accomplished in the world. This is an expression of Your Why. Expose this to yourself. When you expose them to yourself, you realize how you are responding to life's current experiences with the tools and emotions of your past. You may be putting other labels onto your choices and blaming others rather than recognizing the error in your mindset.

"If you cannot be corrected without being offended, you will never grow in life." -Unknown

When others tell you that you have hurt them, it is typical to get offended or defensive. Especially when it is not our intention to harm. Yet the determination of harm is up to the recipient, not the intentions of the offender. Your Why is not an excuse to act any way you choose. Your Why is a motivator to resolve conflict, protect your mind and mood, and promote a productive mindset. You must find the keys to momentum rather than the temptation to defend.

Self-Affirmation K.E.Y.S.

I remember misplacing my car keys last summer while on vacation, or so I thought. As I was preparing to leave the house, I picked up keys that I thought were mine. Once in the car, I realized that I had grabbed my husband's keys and not mine. When we arrived back home from vacation, I looked through every bag and his car to see if my keys had fallen somewhere. For an entire month I didn't drive my car as that was the only set of car keys for my vehicle. I lost my keys and the ones we had (my husband's) were not the right keys for *my* car.

Many of us present as a perfectly functioning 'vehicle' (hair, nails, clothes, all on point) but can't identify why we are not able to move forward. We can't even get our 'vehicle' started. Have you lost your keys, sis? Examine your keys. Examine your Why and how it fits and defines your mindset. Faced with the realization that you don't have the proper keys; you must adjust and shift. You are stuck. Please don't confuse stillness and being stuck. Stillness is a choice to regain peace, sanity. Stuck is an accident of circumstance. We don't choose to be stuck but many of us are. Allow me to present the keys to a healthy mindset— one that gets you unstuck. Knowledge, Endurance, Yield, and Synergize. Find the keys that will get you moving forward.

Knowledge. Trauma can leave a chemical mark on a person's genes. This recently developed area of scientific inquiry is called epigenetics. It suggests that trauma responses are passed down to future generations. This knowledge informs your mindset. The application of your keys may vary based on these preconditions. Your basic instincts and physical reactions may not even be your fault. Yet I am here to tell you to take responsibility and ownership of *how* you move forward. Make it your responsibility to continue to gain knowledge that supports your actions to heal, recover, and *recalibrate*.

Endurance. Power lives within a testimony so don't be selfish with it; but be careful not to use it as a crutch, the thing that is used to gain sympathy and excuse you from moving forward and elevating to your next level. You don't deserve that, so do better for *you*! Too many of us are seeking a quick fix when what we truly need is transformation. We need reconciliation (which does *not* require reconnection). We need forgiveness and to forgive. We need to understand that our point of view is not the *only* view.

Yield. Many of us present well with what society may deem as "the perfect image," the latest name brand clothes, contoured face, eyebrows just right, the "desired shape" and so on. Yet with all of our carefully curated outward presentation, we are broken within. When it is time to drive, you are stuck. You lack the needed tools to thrive, to heal, to execute your vision and dreams. Some of us are riding in 2020 Range Rovers with 1987 Ford Taurus interior (figuratively for those that are very literal.) Yielding is accepting that you don't have the right keys. You may not be well right now, but you are choosing to seek wellness.

You cannot move toward wellness until you accept that your keys are not a fit for your Why, your environment, and your context. Our **keys** to life are much like our car keys. We really can't move forward without them. Sure, your car can be towed from point A to point B but you relinquish your control when that's done. Sure, you can always catch a ride or public transportation, but you can't always be clear of the destination and the timeliness or guarantee of the arrival.

Synergize. Some may have at one point had the keys but somewhere along the journey, they were misplaced, taken from you without your permission, or just neglected. I want every one of you to look around, dig deep, and find your keys. You may not even know they were misplaced, or you have been able to cruise along with your current set but at times, your vehicle locks up. It's time for an evaluation.

How we choose to operate after the loss or after the misplacement and displacement. After the trauma and after the abuse, breakup, embarrassment, after the diagnosis and after the job loss, after the death, and after the judgment, we must choose to rise or sink. We have the power and control of our reactions AND our responses. Stop reacting and learn to respond. This is synergy. Choose peace over pettiness. Peace is worth so much more than the temporary enjoyment pettiness brings. We just need to reshape our mindsets so that our responses propel us rather than inhibit us. What happened to you is not your fault or your responsibility. What you do to recover heal and grow from what happened is on you.

Without your keys, you can't move forward. Without your keys, you will have to get a jump and pay extra, and tag along somebody else's ride. Find your keys and make sure they're tailored to your vehicle, your spiritual, your emotional, your mental. Find your keys.

In some cases, you may never be able to find them so you have to invest in replacing them with keys that are suited for you. They must to be tailor-cut and fit just for you, but it will cost you. I can't tell you what or how much but there's a cost!!! But once the investment is made, you can then begin to move forward. There may be some bumpy roads but you have the tools to keep moving forward, you may get caught at a red light followed by a stop sign and then a train track, but just remember that you're moving forward because you ensured you had the keys.

Bet on yourself.

Ladies, you can't wear a crown with your head down. It'll shift out of position or slip off. Identify your K.E.Y.S. With your head held high and take your royal crown because YOU are Her Majesty.

Reflection Questions

1. What are you going to do with your pain?
2. How are you going to shape and mold it?
3. Which parts of it will you allow to fuel your passion and encourage and bless someone else?

Chapter 8
Getting Your "But" Out of the Way

Universal Law

What you speak into the universe, God or whatever higher power you prescribe to is a powerful call. You not only attract what you speak, you must put the work behind your words. Speak | Believe | Do. That's the recipe. The law of attraction is an automatic magnetic force and the action and effort you put forward is critical to your achievement. When you speak, you are beckoning the outcomes from your higher power. The things that you cannot control, the favor you receive from people, the actions of other people are the result of the law of attraction. You must then respond to confirm and fulfill what you expect to receive from that universal offering.

For example, you speak out into the universe that you would love to connect with a powerful woman, an influencer in women's ministry. You cannot control how that connection occurs. You can write a post on social media and tag the influencer in that post. If you receive a message or a share from that influencer, it is up to you to follow up with that interaction. The offering from God, Allah, ancestors or the universe is an opportunity, tool, and energy. You must respond with work that is faith, will, and consistency. The skill in the application of the law of attraction is an interpretation of the offering and the work response.

You may say that you want a new car. It will not drop from the sky. The opportunity, tools, and energy will be revealed to you. You set the intention with your words. You may put it on a vision board. You continue to put in the work. You remain faithful in the belief of your opportunity. You apply your will to utilize the tools and develop new skills. You nurture positive and progressive energy consistently engaging in intentional interaction. Speak | Believe | Do.

How Big is Your "But"?

In several cultures, the size of one's behind/butt, especially women, equates to wealth and privilege or lack thereof. Many in the American culture view big butts as sexy and admirable. The preference you have is fine.

Why am I bringing this up, and what does any of this have to do with pulling through to your next? The type of but that holds no value and only deters us from our next and should be reduced/eliminated is the "but" that comes so easily when we are trying to make moves. The other day I was talking to my husband about different life plans and our separate and collaborative goals.

He was talking about how he was cleaning and sanitizing everything in the kitchen after he finished working from home that particular day and the last item was the pot. He placed the pot in the sink and told me that he thought to himself "Let me just wash it now because that pot could represent a larger issue or something I may not want to do later on." As he reiterated this example of reducing procrastination, pursuing our goals, and preparing for our next, I got it. I caught that message and said in my Destiny way "yassss, that's a word right there! That'll preach!" Although I was being humorous, I honestly believe that that pot symbolized the very minuscule but important tasks that we push off until later, or sometimes never. Leaving that one thing now could be a major issue, later, even detrimental to your future success(es) down the line. Although at that moment, he was exhausted and didn't feel like it, he *chose* to not use his 'but'. Our 'buts' can block us from moving forward and prevent us from opportunities that we hadn't even dreamt about. How many times have you sat down to write out your vision, or complete a report and you were all prepared? You had the setup, your coffee, good lighting, and your laptop up. Oh yea, it was going to be a productive night. Have you ever been right at the point where you were about to begin researching to prepare a report or detailing your vision plan and you yawn for about 30 seconds? You sit again and look at the laptop and you stare at the screen for about 5 minutes. Maybe you begin writing a sentence or two but then, nothing. The phone may ring, or a Facebook alert pops up. You may continue into those distractions or you may even let your tiredness take over and think to yourself "I really need to get this done BUT I can just do it in the morning. I really want to get this done BUT I'm exhausted." So, the question I want to ask you is how big is your "but"? Is your "but" worth your goals and success? How much does it weigh?

Many times, it seems as though we give our 'buts' more power than we give our plans. The "but" you choose at the moment can block the execution of your vision and delay the implementation of your goals and dreams. Are you allowing your but to hold that much weight to block you from your next?

When It Does Not Work

For those that have faith in the law of attraction and have practiced consistently without results, I first want to assess what you are giving out. The proposition is not transactional. It is not you giving 3 days of good behavior. The law of attraction is not a reward, but a response to consistency. Life tests you. The universe responds to the consistent energy you offer. The universe can offer closed doors while it offers open windows. Your image of what you want your blessing to look like must not limit your openness.

When you say that you are not receiving anything back, what exactly did you expect? You may not have the vehicle you meditated on, but you have the tools and knowledge to build towards it. The steps you receive tailored to you are valuable. You waste it when you refuse the opportunities, tools, and energy because it didn't come in the package you expected it to come in. Again, the skillful application of the law of attraction is to remain open to the responses that the universe provides in specifically the way that the universe provides.

When you observe a person who succeeds, you only see the wins. You may not see the story of trauma, lack, victimhood, and survival. Especially on social media, you either have the success or the completely despairing dark cloud. You must remain open to the full story and also the fact that multiple ways exist to get from point A to point B.

Sometime last year I saw a video that Will Smith posted on Facebook about how he made his big television debut and landed his television series. This happened during a very tough time in his life, struggling financially but also famous. While at the Arsenio Hall show, he meets Benny Medina (who the Fresh Prince is based on) and pitches the idea of the show. Medina introduced him to Quincy Jones at his house, during a celebrity event. They ask Will to do an on-the-spot audition. Will wasn't comfortable with this because he wasn't prepared. Catch that. He had all the key players there and he wasn't prepared and was ready to pass this opportunity now. Quincy said "We can schedule a meeting out for 1 week, but you know what's going to happen?   Something is going to come up. We could do it 3 weeks from now or you can take 10 minutes right now and change your life forever." Will decided to perform right then and there for 10 minutes. Everyone applauds. Quincy asked Brandon Tartikoff, head of NBC, if he liked what he saw and when he said yes, he then asked Will if he had a lawyer to which he responded "no." Quincy assigned him a lawyer and told Brandon and the new attorney to draft up that he's his lawyer and to draw up a new deal for the Fresh Prince of Bel Air right then and there. On the spot. Three months later, the pilot for the Fresh Prince was shot. This all began from his girlfriend at the time telling him he needed to be in the *atmosphere* of where people are doing it. Go to the Arsenio Hall show. She was telling him that if he would just be in the *presence* of greatness.....in the atmosphere, everything else would fall into place. He just had to be there and put in the work. There's a purpose for every person in your life. His relationship with that woman eventually ended but she was in his life for the right time and provided advice that changed his life, and probably hers, for generations to come.....all he had to do was say yes, show up, and perform. Make sure that you're not the weapon formed against yourself causing you not to prosper. Just like Will, that risk you're afraid to take could change your life for the better.

Speaking of risks, almost all life progressions require risk. Get comfortable with the unknown. Get comfortable with ambiguity. You will not always know everything or see the full picture. But that is not required. You only need to know the next step. Seek, learn, and remain ready to take that next step as it is revealed.

Reflection Questions

1. What are you putting into the universe or praying for? What are you expecting from the God or the universe?
2. What is your response when you feel that you are ignored or doors seem to close on you? Have you explored how closed doors may still leave open windows of opportunity, tools, and energy?
3. How have your responses to disappointments contributed to your negativity, conditions, or transactional limiting of the law of attraction?

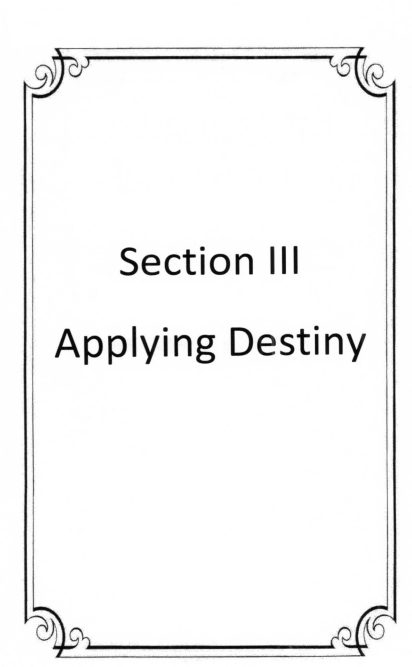

Section III

Applying Destiny

Chapter 9
Ingesting and Digesting

What you ingest physically, spiritually, emotionally, and mentally is what you provide to your wholeness and wellbeing to digest. Admittedly, others may have lacked in the area of affirming you. They provided you with a blueprint for despair, trepidation, and imposter syndrome. You consumed that negativity possibly through no fault of your own growing up and/or into adulthood. But, ask yourself whether you are continuing that diet. You are what you eat. Take a look at what you are consuming.

- What is your core circle of people?

- What are you reading?

- What music do you listen to?

- What are you eating for your physical health?

- What are you doing to aid your circulation, digestion, and elimination?

Your body, mind, and spirit will conform to what you ingest. You may know a person who has chosen veganism who takes a break and consumes a burger. They most likely will have a reaction through their digestion because their body has become used to only processing fruits and vegetables. You become what you digest in the same way. When you go backward after eliminating negativity from your diet, negativity troubles your soul. When you become equally yoked with the positivity, progress, and power in life, you edify your mind, body, and spirit.

Changing Environment

If you are surrounded by what got you sick, how do you become well? When we assess our physical wellness plan, we often become concerned only when something is wrong. A healthy workout regimen or an improved diet is motivated by a diagnosis or feelings of sluggishness. With diabetes, you may change your sugar intake. With heart trouble, you may seek the help of a doctor or nutritionist. Our spiritual, emotional, and mental wellness plan will often come from a "diagnosis" from people you care about. Your friend may suggest, "Destiny, why did you go off like that over something so small?" That is a subtle wake-up call that you need to heal rather than become defensive.

Sometimes, the precursor is a motivation within—a question or desire for change within. You may just be tired of being tired. You may want something different from life than what you have been receiving. In short, your "diagnosis" as it were, may be external or internal. Externally, you may be losing friends. Internally, you may feel a need for change. The goals are:

- To gain a sense of our own choice in situations.
- To exercise a choice for freedom (being unstuck).
- To create a sense of being equally yoked within (mind, body, and spirit).

Choice. It is often easy to place the blame on others. That is because it seems justified. Yet, even if you have been shown otherwise, you have to own your decision making. In that admonishment, you take your power back. Your responsibility from that point is to share your process with others. Determine how you are going to be a catalyst and change the trajectory for others who appear powerless and bound. Once we empower ourselves, we must empower others. The result is your freedom. The return on that investment or the confirmation of your journey is the influence on others.

Freedom. Healing is the first step. Spiritual, emotional, and mental bondage is a state of being held captive to the guilt and shame we feel about the choices we have made. Being unstuck doesn't propel you forward necessarily. You can be still even when you are free. Stillness is an opportunity to plan, gather yourself, and create. That process is important especially during your healing process. Being stuck is usually not conducive to planning, gathering, or creating. Stuck is a place of repeating bad choices because they provide temporary relief from a life of bondage. Healing begins as you stop and adjust what we fuel ourselves with. Bring your stress level down. Exercise your freedom to make different choices for your long-term benefit rather than temporary relief.

Equally Yoked. Traditionally, a discussion of being equally yoked from a Biblical context means connecting with a person that shares a similar path to yours. Often, it means choosing someone who believes in the same religion as you. Individually, I see equally yoked as an internal task. Your physical, mental, and spiritual must be in balance. Most people live for others and focus on the physical making our body look right for others. The commentary is evident daily. The evaluation is always about how others will see you. The makeup, the mask, or the deception we portray doesn't hide our character as it is expressed in action. The made-up person can still flip tables as they do on reality shows. If you cater your media, relationship, and support diets to edifying sources, you can choose balance and achieve it. Your energy will be different.

Your task is not to "become worthy." You are worthy. The task is to act upon that reality. Worthiness is often correlated with value. You are valuable in whatever space you are in. The influences around you may cause you to feel less than, but you do not need to reach a certain level to be valuable. You only need to reach for your choice, freedom, and become equally yoked within.

The last 10 years of my life I've helped everyone else thrive; I've supported and pushed others' dreams and visions while shelving my own. Did I feel that I was failing? No. But I definitely felt like I was coasting. Just doing everything to be the best friend, sister, daughter, wife, mother, colleague, Godmother. But I neglected me. I neglected the idea of dreaming and jumping because I allowed myself to thrive off of and be fulfilled by the pride and joy I genuinely felt when another woman wins. I'm happy to have played a part in helping them execute their vision. But the problem was, I laid mine to the side more and more until I just let my vision sit for days, months, then years. They never died but they were neglected. But let me tell you... the resuscitation of my vision has been activated and I've not only seen the power illuminate from within, but I've also seen some that I have supported, empowered, uplifted, nursed, and dropped things for, be the last one to say any type of "you go girl" or "okay I see you Des! Keep doing your thing!" Am I looking for that? No. Does that support and encouragement from others, especially those you went above for seem like an expected friend response?

Of course. But once you learn to truly be free from needing or expecting the validation of anyone outside of God and yourself, you will truly be unbothered, more aware and cautious of how much energy you're willing to give out without having any of it poured back into you. Remember reciprocity. I made the mistake that far too many of us make as nurturers, lovers, and helpers- depleting yourself for others at the expense of your peace, energy, and space. Sis, I want freedom for you, by any means necessary.

Your Foundation

Create a new foundation of people, places, and things. You can often see the hopelessness and despair in the eyes of others even with the front that they attempt to portray. The smiles, makeup, jokes, and other attempts at appearances are not able to hide a badly hurting heart. Consider that the tasks of choice, freedom, and being equally yoked are tasks for circulation and elimination.

Your foundation can be solid rock or sinking sand. Solid rock is a foundation that allows you to build your true strength. You find wholeness and healing that allows you to snap back even after several failures and disappointments. There are times when you will ingest things that are not the most beneficial for you. Yet, healing is about having the tools to process the experiences and get rid of what is a challenge to you or does not benefit you. It is like receiving a vaccine. Once you take the vaccine, exposure to the virus will not take you down in the same way as when you have not had the vaccine. The healing is your solid foundation.   In the same way epigenetics can result in negative outcomes, you can create a foundation that supports a positive legacy for you, your children, and your children's children. Be the facilitator of generational blessings and healing. Review your roots and foundation. Where things aren't sturdy and firm, it is time to rebuild, reconstruct, and renew.

Circulation. Basically, what you take in will come out. The good is kept as food digests, and the waste is eliminated. That is the normal process. That is the physical level. It works the same on a spiritual and emotional level. What you accept, view, and interact with is processed at a spiritual and emotional level. When you operate within the world, you are aware of what you have ingested.

You maintain circulation through a wellness diet. You must tailor the plan for you. Each person requires a specific/unique wellness plan. It could be Bible reading, Reiki, yoga, meditation or ASMR that is your "equally yoked" diet. Just like a doctor may allow some to have certain foods and forbid it from others, you may be able to view some television drama or you may need to refuse all drama. I cannot tell you what to do, but the goal you have identified is the priority.

Continually circulate to activate the power of flow.

The damage of a blockage can be devastating. Consistency is the key to your success. Build your habits around ingesting a positive diet and maintaining flow. You know whether you are striking the right balance because we know the results of flow. When you are ingesting and benefitting from the positive, positivity will flow out of you. Self-reflection is vital to your becoming.

Elimination. You are going to release what you nurture within your body. Adults often ask how a teenager learns their negative behaviors. The answer is simple for me. They are releasing what has been their diet. Your intention doesn't matter as much as your diet does. Think about it: when you ingest certain vitamins or drink a particular vegetable juice;

your urine may change color due to what you are eating. Your lifestyle, interactions, and spirituality respond similarly. If you feed yourself with negativity, drama, and strife, you will release that same venom onto those that are in your immediate proximity. Often, you release upon those that you care about the most. You are the determinant, based on what you ingest and what is digested.

When you release, you are releasing energy and momentum into the atmosphere. When you say, "I'm going to always be broke," the universe does not know the difference between your joke or idle comment and how it should operate. You are forming a weapon against yourself. You are condemning yourself. You must reform your habits. You must also feed those habits with the appropriate progressive and positive food. Intentionally perform an exit examination for yourself after each interaction, when goals are accomplished, and when you are tasked with reloading.

Reflection Questions

1. How are you detoxing and refueling your affirmation, edification, and progress?
2. How do you check in to assess your circulation and elimination?
3. What choices can you intentionally make to move from being stuck to being still?

Chapter 10
Speaking Destiny

Speak Destiny is a process of Transformation, Empowerment, Affirmation, Confirmation, Healing. TEACH if you will. More than just a great acronym, TEACH helps you remember how to speak to yourself and how to speak destiny into your life. Begin with recognizing your glow.

Transforming and Emphasizing Your Glow: The TEACH Model

Your glow doesn't come from external factors, it begins from within: healing, love, happiness, and soul work. Training your mind and shifting your perspective results in wholeness as well as wealth and achievement. Often, women have learned to take pride in our suffering for the benefit of others whether for our kids, man, family, and sometimes friends. Struggle mentality tends to be praised but healing, wholeness, and fulfillment are being neglected and rejected. Meanwhile, your wholeness will provide greater benefit to those in your life. The more health you embody, the more health you exude.

The opposite of the struggle mentality is the queendom mentality. Queendom mentality, or as I like to call it Femtality, comes with a glow. Dedication, involvement, work ethic, and productivity increase and are visible and energetic when you are whole.

Better or broken are the possible outcomes but they are also choices. You accept that your past has happened. What happened is not a reflection of you nor is it your identity. You are not at fault for what happened. However, you are responsible for what you do next. Trauma brokenness is when you sit, stuck in the experience of your trauma. The trauma does impact you, but it doesn't have to define (stifle) you. If you are like many, you spend a great deal of time defending yourself. You make sure that others know that you have been through something. You need to validate your story. BUT the story should not end there. Trauma Recovery is a choice to respond to trauma as if it is a motivation to move forward. Trauma necessitates a new way of speaking to yourself and interacting with others.

Transformation. Speaking transformation means that you cease to speak in the now and what you don't have. Speak what you want to have as if it is present. Speak gratitude for the things that you do have. Acknowledge what is positive and progressive at the moment. Reframe your thought of the present into what you want it to be.

Rather than, "I wish I was thinner. I just lost my job. I'm broke."

Speak instead, "I am living a healthy lifestyle. Thank God for sustaining me and my family. I am progressing toward my goals every day."

Empowerment. Now that you have the tools, you must go and TEACH. You must help others. You know that others are choosing anger, greed, and despair. You activate your healing through your service. In speaking to them, you allow them to borrow your strength until they can build enough for themselves. It's a concept from Lisa Nichols that she presented in her book *No Matter What.*

"You will be able to purchase that car. You will be a homeowner. You will overcome your barriers."

Affirmation. This is your main speaking regimen. You must speak in the affirmative concerning your future goals. Put reminders up around your house. Just like when learning a song, an effective method is by repetition, do the same for your goals. Rehearse what can be there and reshape what is through your repetitive speech.

"I am enough. I am worthy. I will be respected. I provide value. I am confident. I am loved. I am beautiful. I am worth it. I am changing. I am growing. I am becoming."

Confirmation. This is the cap on your affirmation. It is a reflection or assessment of your achievement in a moment. It is similar to affirmation but adds evidence to measure your progress. You can adjust what you are doing to meet your standard and accept your process of healing.

Notice the progress you have made. Review the baseline and what the mirror showed you when you started, compared to now. Write that down on one side of a sheet of paper. On the other side, respond with how each situation has been resolved or the effort you have put into the process of healing.

Speak confirmation in phrases like, "I made progress in [this] area." Speak directly to the [this] that you wrote on the paper. Only you can evaluate yourself. Be kind. Be patient. And continue to move forward at your own pace.

Healing. Your healing is seen in the context of your service to yourself. The benefits extend beyond self. For example, a good employee helps the company, but they gain in the process as well. You cannot be the best mother, wife, friend if you are not the best for you! Continue to choose to prioritize yourself, your journey, your destiny. Your story helps shape you but your story does not define you nor does it end in a dark space.

"I am healing. I am willing to be stretched and challenged. My story is ongoing. I can begin again. My process is adding jewels to my crown."

Intentional Action: The Pull Up Femtality

(I wrote this portion in a new Women's Magazine *Her Hustle Magazine* which I recommend you subscribe to or add to your list).

Everything we gain in life is for the greater good, not just for ourselves. The power in knowledge can't be quantified and spreading it amongst other women unites us and empowers other women who may otherwise feel powerless. We must give back, as it's our responsibility.

I remember my son and I watching the classic, "The Land Before Time" which is one of my childhood faves. My five-year-old at the time commented about Cera (Triceratops) and Littlefoot (Apatosaurus) arguing and fighting with each other. He couldn't understand why these dinosaurs were fighting each other when their goal was the same—to find the Great Valley. He said, "That's crazy. They should not be fighting because they're the same. They're both dinosaurs. Why is she being so mean to him?" I explained to him that she (Cera), just like some people, had so much pain bottled up within, that manifested into anger due to her circumstances (getting separated from family and being alone) that she projected her feelings towards others, even while they were trying to help her. Sound familiar? Is this someone you know? Is this you?

My son's comment and questioning stuck with me. I thought specifically about women and our interactions with one another. We are the same in so many ways, but we often spend more energy in competition rather than collaboration. We identify how one type of woman is better than the other, whether by status, finances, beauty, physique, or personality. It is imperative for us as women to not only build one another up but that we learn from one another and pull each other up once we are equipped with the tools and skills to pass on. When we learn, grow and evolve, very little of it is just for us.

The greatest way to show our weaknesses and insecurities is to keep our gifts for ourselves. We can't be selfish with our gifts. The gift or calling on you can't be taken from you, even when you share it with others. Your knowledge and expertise can never be diminished when you share them with other women. The only thing that can happen is that they evolve based on the seed YOU planted. Once they grow and evolve, they will have learned to do the same. See how that works? It becomes a cycle, the norm. We need to create a sense of normalcy around empowerment. The only way we all make it is to help pull others up in our journey. The Pull Up Femtality.

Winning Together

My two little cousins were playing the Game of Perfection. One took her chance and began the game. She could not complete it in time. The other attempted, but she also could not do it alone. For a third game, they chose to work together. They completed the task before the time limit.

We can work solo, but when we come together, we win. I always say collaboration over competition. I promote togetherness that proposes to reach more women rather than segmenting the audience. My vision is varied. Fempreneurs (female entrepreneurs) areas of expertise do not necessarily work hand-in-hand, but you know what can be done? Women from all walks of life can connect and pour into one another. For example, a fempreneur in real estate can promote the work and expertise of a motivational speaker who can empower her team, thus increasing sales. This is collaboration. This is mutual support. When we recognize that one woman's win is also our win, we will realize the power of collaboration over competition. The joy on the face of other women, specifically black women when Regina King won her Golden Globe was palpable and an example of the spirit of mutual achievement. She also won the Academy Award that year. Her win was their win. Her win was a win for all of us.

Imagine how long it would take for a dynamic community of women to individually progress without the wisdom, collaboration, or insight from someone who's trotted that path not too long ago. Now imagine how long it would take for the same dynamic community of women to progress with the blueprint, resources, and assistance that may or may not have been available to you? We should always want the next generation of women to have better opportunities and fewer obstacles that we may have faced along our journey of becoming. Please don't confuse what I'm saying with becoming someone's bank and funding their lives while they make unwise or frivolous decisions. I am speaking of providing the tools for success that were instrumental in our success. Resilience, growth mindset, financial literacy, mentorship, investing. You won't lose your fire or following when you give back and invest in other women. If you're the woman who currently holds the torch, I don't ask that you pass it, I ask that you assist another woman or rather a community of women with building their own torches using some of your materials. Once they've created their rendition of a torch, light it with **_your_** fire. An entire community of women can have lit torches from your **single** flame. See how that works? I do this not only in my business, Speak Destiny, but in all aspects of my daily life. Lighting others' torches. My flame won't diminish when I light your torch, nor will it dim when you then light the torch of ten other women. The flame continues to extend. I salute you woman. Keep striving, keep reaching, keep excelling, but most importantly, don't forget to go back and pull others up along your journey.

Reflection Questions

1. What gifts are you withholding that others are waiting on?
2. Can you identify moments where you projected your pain onto others around you?
3. How do you light the torch for other women and shine your light?

Chapter 11
The Forty-Five Days

Commit to Speak Destiny over the next 45 days. You have the first practical activity. TEACH. Allow me to present the second practice: REACH.

Women Must R.E.A.C.H.

R-eflect on the areas in your life that you've neglected. The situations that you've suppressed or buried. Reflect on the challenges and the intention to overcome them. Reflect on your journey and how you overcame past obstacles. Reflect on the experiences that you would like to release and be freed from.

E-dify yourself with books, professional developments, trainings, mentorship, retreats, spa days, and self-care. All of these are necessary to the empowerment of your mind, body, and soul.

A-ccountability, taking ownership when things aren't executed properly and when you have offended someone even if unintentional. Be teachable from anyone regardless of title and apologize when mistakes are made. It is important that you encourage others to hold you accountable. It's beneficial for your growth.

C-hange is critical. You must be able to adjust and remain flexible. Move with the "cheese" or become molded and extinct. Assess and identify issues and adjust accordingly. Sometimes this change looks like changing your circle or adjusting your tribe. Change looks like not addressing situations in the same manner you once did in the past. Change is critical to your growth.

H-umility is imperative. Remain humble. Be able to listen and also follow those with wisdom. You don't know it all; it's impossible.   Don't take things personally. When you meet certain milestones and goals, don't ever begin looking down on others but rather bring others up with you. Help pull others up. This is how the growth cycle continues and brings about change within communities.

Now to begin your 45-day journey, please make sure you have a journal to 'journal your journey' as my father says. This will allow you to not only track but also reflect on your progress. Your first 15 days will involve reflection and learning around the TEACH model. This will be your task for the first 15 days. Feed your freedom and a new narrative intentionally through practicing each letter of the acronyms and celebrating your progress as you Speak Destiny.

The next 15 days will focus on your REACH. To change, you must move forward through the discomfort that naturally occurs when we learn and stretch toward something new. The most monumental activity in TEACH and REACH involves your interactions with others. For TEACH, it is empowerment and sharing of your tools and learning. For REACH, it is the humility in practice that suggests that you reach out to people who have hurt you in the search for peace.

Transparency moment. Whew. I was dating someone before college who displayed a lot of insecurities and attachment dependency. As I left for college, he was worried that I would meet someone and forget about him. I was not going to limit or shrink my dreams for another person's needs or wants. I ended the relationship and became free from his threats and any other reactions.

I had moved on. I was in another relationship and was still receiving non-stop calls (over 100 within 2 hours) back-to-back. It was so excessive, my pink Palm Centro crashed, continuously restarting, and freezing.

For context, out of all the many losses I have experienced in life, losing my best friend at the age of 14 was the most traumatic for me. Still is. I would relive good times in my dreams and wake up to reality.

When I finally picked up to ask him to cease the calls since now my phone was acting up, he said, "You are making a mistake. I had a dream about your best friend, and he told me that he would not visit you in your dreams anymore if you left me. You would be a bad friend to him if you left me!" He attempted to use this memory and connection as a dagger against me. This is a person who had prayed with and for my best friend while he was in the hospital and even lived with my family when I left home. It broke me at the moment. My boyfriend at the time (now my husband) saw me trying to quietly hide my pain as tears streamed down my face. I wasn't angry or mad. I was hurt, sad, and actually surprised. There had been several previous and post relationship painful acts that had occurred as well. However, none stung as deep as this.

Fast forward more than decade later, I reached out to him out of nowhere. This pain and resentment had been rising within me, on and off, over the years, especially whenever the memory of my best friend was spoken of. He called back and asked what was up. I told him that I was doing my soul work and addressing things from my past that hurt me and needed to forgive and also heal from. I told him that it still hurts. He apologized. "I was so young and broken myself. I could not positively express myself. I thought going that low would force you into being with me." I appreciated that he took responsibility for his actions and owned everything. I know this will not be the experience of everyone. But that helped me in this instance. He told me that he had been going through old emails and felt that he should reach out. He was hesitant, not knowing whether I would be receptive which shocked me. He had been feeling the need to apologize first and address this 10+ year old situation? I was surprised and relieved. Even if the interaction does not go the way you hope, your sincere effort to reach is rewarded with a peace that allows you to move on. The experience was truly healing for me.

The weight lifted means that you feel less anxious in those moments where you may be triggered. You may be in conversations with people who are connected to the person. You can own your voice, your feelings, and your opportunities to move forward. Peace is practical in that you are no longer hindered consciously or subconsciously. You can hold your head high in all situations without hesitation. I want you to know that progress, change, and growth benefits from your decision and action to reach out. I struggled with choosing to share this specific experience with you but as I noted earlier, it's our responsibility to share our journey, our story, with other women to help them through and see that it does work. It is possible. And even if the person(s) who have wronged you don't own it or apologize, or even if they are deceased, freedom still awaits you when you release it and forgive. You deserve freedom sis.

Keep Being a Pedal Pusher

The change that you make today will determine the trajectory of your life. Will you choose to remain the same and stay comfortable? Or are you going to begin to R.E.A.C.H? If you're unwilling to learn, no one can help you. If you're determined to learn, no one, absolutely no one can stop you! Sis, I am rooting for you to R.E.A.C.H.

A couple of years ago, my husband and I took our son to the park to ride his tricycle and just get some fresh air. The weather was surprisingly nice for mid-October in Maryland. Well, as he was riding around on the sidewalk, he didn't seem to have any issues. It wasn't until the pathway began to incline which caused him to have to put a little more effort in. Well, actually a lot more effort. While he was pedaling and trying his best to go up the hill, he told us that he needed help. My husband told him something so very small and obvious that resonated with me. He said "Joseph if you stop pedaling while you are going up the hill, it'll make it harder. You have to keep pushing, keep pedaling. If you stop you will start going back and have to start again." I don't know if it was the creative side of my brain kicking in but I agreed immediately saying "yasss! Now that's a word right there!!" I took out my phone, went to the notepad app, and copied down what had just transpired.

I thought about the hundreds of youths I have worked with throughout the years, all leading different lives and different dreams, but with the same goal, to succeed and complete the job training program which for many also included earning their GED or high school diploma. Completing looks different for many. For some, it means leaving to work in their career field. For others, it means enlisting into the military. For another, college is the next step. Whatever the "next" level is, they knew the importance of moving forward and upward. Stopping couldn't be an option-they had way too much to lose. Too much baggage behind. Too much negativity could pull them back into the trauma that they had escaped and were healing from.

I want you to know that even though going up this hill that you're facing is tougher than riding the flat surface, keep trucking. Pedal harder. Keep moving. If you look back while going, you will swerve off course. If you stop pedaling for a break, you may begin to reverse without intending to. Keep pushing sis! Keep going to your next. You got this! You can do it! Keep reminding yourself that daily. And when you get to the top of that hill, you can scope out the view, assess your surroundings, determine what you need and what you don't, rest, and then continue for greater. What do these inclines symbolize in your life? A promotion, paying off debts, preparing to purchase a home, preparing for marriage, filing for divorce, forgiving your abuser, starting your own business? Whatever your 'next' is, remember, don't take your foot off the pedal.

Permission to Build

Your third last 15 days of the process will be spent Growing: Becoming Comfortable Being Uncomfortable. You have permission to build. With that, I want you to give yourself permission to fall and stumble while building. You cannot expect to build a house without any issues, setbacks, or challenges. Healing will be messy. You are excavating hidden, dangerous, and treacherous areas. This is not a microwavable process. You Speak Destiny as a continuous process. Your rewards will not occur overnight. Know that. Recognize the process as a motivator of gratitude. Trust the process.

You will always be stretched while improving. You will sometimes backtrack, but you will always point in the right direction. No matter how many times you stumble, you will move toward your goal, if you *choose* to. You may have felt fixed in your mindset, stuck in your ways or situation, locked into a destiny. But I want you to know that you must TEACH and REACH continually. This doesn't end after the 45-day process however, it should become less of a task and more of the norm, forming a habit, after the 45 days.

You may have gotten used to getting your results immediately. I remember when dial-up Internet took hours to download songs and burn them to a CDROM. Fellow millennials, I know you feel my pain. Now, we can click on a song on our phones and hear it almost instantly. The treatment plan is to rehearse this for the rest of your life. Understand that this is life. Stick to your diet, your practice, your healing. Even as you feel better, see improvement and reach your desired goals, continue to Speak Destiny.

A person who wins an Academy Award doesn't hang up acting and fire their acting coach. They up their game now knowing what it takes to build to a certain level. They are primed to the next level. You are no different. TEACH and get to the next level. REACH and continue to lead. Continue to Speak Destiny.

Reflection Questions

1. What is the meaning behind your behavior?
2. What is the meaning behind the behaviors of those that have impacted you when you deserved loving behaviors?
3. Who do you need to forgive in order to become free?

About the Author

Destiny Hilliard-Thomas is an author, mindset & purpose coach, educator, therapist and speaker with a passion for helping others achieve their full potential. As the founder of Speak Destiny, she's on a mission to unite with her clients and empower them to embrace their true selves and reach goals they once thought impossible. Through sharing key tools and strategies, Destiny hopes to inspire her readers to cultivate a growth mindset, find their purpose, and create lifelong positive change. Destiny holds a Master's degree in counseling from John Hopkins University and a Bachelor's degree in education from Hampton University. For more information, visit: SpeakDestiny.com or follow @ispeakdestiny on Facebook, Instagram and LinkedIn.

About the Book

Speak Destiny: A Powerful Path to Embrace Your True Self, Overcome Negativity, and Find Your Freedom is a powerful and heartfelt book designed to help women everywhere discover how to embrace their true selves, cultivate emotional and mental wellbeing, and create their ideal lives. With a heartfelt exploration of the societal pressures, harmful mindsets, and emotional burdens which hold readers back, this book is a gem; and inside you'll find a practical selection of techniques for transforming your mindsets and overcoming whatever challenges you face.

Covering how to accept yourself with honesty and vulnerability, how to practice forgiveness, how to free yourself from negative mindsets through positive self-talk and affirmations, and so much more, *Speak Destiny* provides readers with a proven roadmap for spiritual, emotional, and mental wellness. Plus, with a 45-day plan to help you implement everything you learn, this gem of a book is perfect for any woman who wants to discover her true potential and live her best life.

Made in the USA
Middletown, DE
03 July 2021

43568357R00080